UNDERSTANDING NEHEMIAH

A Commentary Using Ancient Bible Study Methods

MICHAEL HARVEY KOPLITZ

Table of Contents

Introduction

While I was attending Seminary earning my M. Div. degree, I started to question what the instructors and reference books were saying about the Scriptures. One of the ideas being offered then was that the Bible was full of errors and not factual. I found that attitude disturbing for Seminary instructors to be teaching. After all, the Seminary experience is to train pastors to go out into God's world and preach the Bible. How can you preach the Bible if you believe what these instructors are teaching? The methods that were being taught to examine the Bible just seemed inaccurate to me.

After graduating from Seminary, I spent much time reading different views about the Bible. I eventually read the Zohar. This collection of Midrashim is considered the secret work of the Torah, according to Kabbalists. Also, I learned quite a bit about Messianic Judaism. Their view of the Bible is quite different from the Seminary view.

I decided that the biblical interpretation that was being taught in the Seminary was not the biblical interpretation the people heard when Jesus Christ (whose Hebraic name is Yeshua) preached. I went on a quest to learn what the people of Yeshua's day thought about Scripture and what they thought when the Scriptures were read. This quest led me to Dr. Anne Davis and The Bible Learning University. Dr. Davis was in search of the same thing I was searching for. She had made many discoveries that helped me in my quest. I earned the Ph. D. degree from The Bible Learning University in Hebraic Studies in Christianity, concentrating on ancient Bible Studies methods.

Finally, I found someone who believed that the church had placed almost 1900 years of theological ideas about the Scriptures and, in many places, possibly distorting its original meaning. What is also vital to hear is that the basic tenants of Yeshua as God's Messiah, my Lord, and Savior are in the Bible. My faith in Yeshua is more vital now that I have learned from Dr. Davis how to study the Scriptures in the same manner that the people did in Yeshua's day.

I have included an article that describes the differences between Greek learning methods and Hebraic learning methods. Please do not skip this chapter unless you are familiar with ancient Bible study methods. If you do, then the analysis and commentary that follows may become difficult for you to understand.

Our God is vast and infinite, and so is His Word. May God bless you in your discovery of what God's Word is about.

Nehemiah was a great leader of Israel and had deep religious convictions. He lived at the Shushan Palace in 465 BCE. Nehemiah had obtained the office of cupbearer to Artakhshisht, King of Persian. This office allowed him to be in the presence of the King daily. Naturally, the princes of the Empire sought this position. Thus, the cupbearer influenced the workings of the Empire. Also, he had inside information. He was the only person allowed to enter and leave the King's throne room at any time.

Nehemiah must have been well educated and a man of integrity and trustworthiness to have been appointed to such an exalted position. No one came into the presence of the King without being summoned. If someone came before the King without an invitation, they could be immediately killed. The King would hold out his scepter if he decided to allow the intruder in (see the story of Esther).

In April 445 CE, Nehemiah was permitted to go to Jerusalem to rebuild the city's walls. He was able to obtain timber for the gates and other building materials that were needed for the rebuilding of the walls. The King granted Nehemiah powers that were never given to a Jew. He could issue orders to the King's army south of the Euphrates River. He also controlled the food supplies and King's treasury in that part of the Empire.

King Cyrus in 538 BCE ordered by edict the rebuilding of Jerusalem and the Temple of the LORD. Many Jews returned to Jerusalem from Exile in Babylon. The enemies of the Jews hampered the work at Jerusalem. The Samaritans and Gentiles of the Galilee, Sanballat[i], Tubiah, and Geshem the Arabian, made every effort to stop the rebuilding of the walls.[1]

---

[1] Rocco A. Errico and George M. Lamsa, *Aramaic Light on Ezra Through the Song of Solomon* (Smyrna, GA: Noohra Foundation, 2010).

The main differences between the Greek method and the Hebraic method of teaching

Once a student becomes aware of these two teaching styles, the student will determine if the class attended or if a book was read, whether the teaching method is either a Greek or Hebraic method. In the Greek manner, the instructor is always right because of advanced knowledge. In the college situation, it is because the Professor has his/her Ph.D. in some area of study, so one assumes that he or she knows everything about the topic. For example, Rodney Dangerfield played the role of a middle-aged man going to college. His English midterm was to write about Kurt Vonnegut Jr. Since he did not understand any of Vonnegut's books, he hired Vonnegut himself to write the midterm. When he received the paper from the English Professor told Dangerfield that whoever wrote the paper knew nothing about Vonnegut. The Professor's words are an example of the Greek method of teaching. Did the Ph.D. English Professor think that she knew more about Vonnegut's writings than Vonnegut did? [2]

In the Greek teaching method, the Professor or the instructor claims to be the authority. If one attends a Bible study class and the class leader says, "I will teach you the only way to understand this biblical book," you may want to consider the implications. This method is standard since most Seminaries and Bible colleges teach a Greek mode of learning, which is the same method the church has been utilizing for centuries.

Hebraic teaching methods are different. The teacher wants the students to challenge what they hear. It is through questioning that a student can learn. The teacher also wants his/her students to excel to a point where the student becomes the teacher.

---

[2] *Back to School.* Performed by Rodney Dangerfield. Hollywood: CA: Paper Clip Productions, 1986. DVD.

If two rabbis come together to discuss a Scripture passage, the result will be at least ten different opinions. All points of view are acceptable if each is supported by biblical evidence. It is permissible and encouraged that students develop many ideas. There is a depth to God's Word, and God wants us to find all His messages contained in the Scripture.

Seeking out the meaning of the Scriptures beyond the literal meaning is essential to understand God's Word fully.[3] The Greek method of learning the Scriptures has prevailed over the centuries. One problem is that only the literal interpretation of Scripture was often viewed as valid, as prompted by Martin Luther's "sola literalis," meaning that just the literal translation of Scripture was accurate. The Fundamentalist movements of today base their beliefs on the literal interpretation of the Scripture. Therefore, they do not believe that God placed more profound, hidden, or secret meanings in the Word.

The students of the Scriptures who learn through Hebraic training and understanding have drawn a different conclusion. The Hebrew language itself leads to different possible interpretations because of the construction of the language. The Hebraic method of Bible study opens avenues of thought about God's revelations in the Scripture never considered. Not all questions about the Scripture studied will have an immediate answer. If so, it becomes the responsibility of the learners to uncover the meaning. Also, remember that many opinions about the meaning of Scripture are also acceptable.

---

[3] Davis, Anne Kimball. *The Synoptic Gospels*. MP3. Albuquerque: NM: BibleInteract, 2012.

Methodology

The methodology employed is to use First Century Scripture study methods integrated with Yeshua's day's customs and culture to examine the Hebrew and Christian Scriptures, thus gathering a more in-depth understanding by learning the Scriptures in the way the people of Yeshua's day did.

I have titled the methodology of analyzing a passage of Scripture in a Hebraic manner the "Process of Discovery." The author developed this methodology, which brings together various areas of linguistic and cultural understanding. There are several sections to the process, and not all the parts apply to every passage of Scripture. The overall result of developing this process is to give the reader a framework for studying the Word in more depth.

The "Process of Discovery" starts with a Scripture passage. An examination of the linguistic structure of the passage is next. The linguistic structure includes parallelism, chiastic structures, and repetition. Formatting the passage in its linguistic form allows the reader to visualize what the first century CE listener was hearing. Their corresponding sections label the chiasms, for example, A, B, C, B', A.' Not all passages of the Scriptures have a poetic form.

The next step is to "question the narrative." The questioning of the narrative process, assuming the reader knows nothing about the passage. Therefore, the questions go from the simple to the complex. The next task is to identify any linguistic patterns. Linguistic patterns include, but are not limited to, irony, simile, metaphor, symbolism, idioms, hyperbole, figurative language, personification, and allegory.

A review of any translation inconsistencies discovered between the English NAU version and either the Hebrew or Greek versions is done. There are times when a Hebrew or Greek word is translated in more than one way. Inconsistencies also can be created by the translation committee, which may have decided to use traditional language instead of the actual translation. The decision of the translation committee is in the Preface or Introduction to the Bible. Perhaps some of the inconsistencies were intentionally added to convey some deeper meaning. An examination for every discrepancy is done.

The passage is analyzed for any echoes of the Hebrew Scriptures in the Christian Scriptures. Using a passage from the Hebrew Scriptures in the Christian Scriptures, an echo occurs.[4] Also, echoes are found when Torah (Genesis through Deuteronomy) passages are used in other Hebrew Bible books. Cross-references in the Scripture are references from one verse to another verse, which can help the reader understand the verse.

The names of persons mentioned in the passage are listed. Many of the Hebrew names have meaning and may be associated with places or actions. Jewish parents used to name their children based on what they felt God had in store for their child. An example of this is Abraham, whose original name was Abram and was changed to mean eternal father (God changed Abram's name to Abraham, indicating a function he was to perform). When the Hebrew Bible gives names, many of the occurrences mean something unique. The same importance can occur for the names of places. The time it takes to travel between locations can supply insight into the event.

---

[4] Mitzvot are the 613 commandments found in the Torah that please God. There are positive and negative commandments. The list was first development by Maimonides. The full list can be found at: ttp://www.jewfaq.org/613.htm.

Keyphrases are identified in verses when they are essential to an understanding of that passage. There are no rules for selecting the keywords. Searching for other occurrences of the keywords in Scripture in a concordance is necessary to understand the Word's usage; this must be done in either Hebrew or Greek, not in English. A classic Hebraic approach is to find the usage of a word in the Scripture by finding other verses that contain the Word. The usage of a word in its original language is discovered by searching the Scripture in the language of the Word. Verses that contain the Word are identified, and a pattern for the usage of the Word is discovered. Each verse is examined to see what the usage of the Word is which, may reveal a model for the Word's usage. For Hebrew words, the first usage of the Word in the Scripture, primarily if used in the Torah, is essential. For the Greek words, the Christian Scriptures are used to determine the Word usage in the Scripture. Sometimes finding the equivalent Greek Word in the Septuagint then analyzing its Hebrew usage can be very helpful.

The Rules of Hillel are used when applicable. Hillel was a Torah scholar who lived shortly before Yeshua's day. Hillel developed several rules for Torah students to interpret the Scriptures, which refer to halachic Midrash. In several cases, these rules are helpful in the analysis of the Scripture.

The cultural implications from the period of the writing are done after the linguistic analysis is completed. The culture is crucial because it is not explicitly referenced in the biblical narratives, as indicated earlier.

From the linguistic analysis and the cultural understanding, it is possible to obtain a deeper meaning of the Scripture beyond the plain text's literal meaning. That is what the listeners of Yeshua's time were doing. They put linguistics and culture together without even having to contemplate it.

The analysis will lead to a set of findings explaining what the passage meant in Yeshua's day. Most of the time, the Hebraic analysis leads to the desire for more in-depth analysis to fully understand what Yeshua was talking about or what was happening to Him. Whatever the result, a new, more in-depth understanding of the Scripture is obtained.

The components of the Process of Discovery are:

Language

  Process of Discovery

    Linguistics Section

      Linguistic Structure

      Discussion

      Questioning the Passage

      Verse Comparison of citations or proof text

      Translation Inconsistencies

      Biblical Personalities

      Biblical Locations

      Phrase Study

      Scripture cross-references

      Linguistic Echoes

      Rules of Hillel

Culture Section

Discussion

Questioning the passage

Cultural Echoes

Culture and Linguistics Section

Discussion

Thoughts

Reflections

Only the applicable sections are included in this document.

Chapter One

Language

New American Standard 1995	Hebrew
Neh. 1:1 The words of [a]Nehemiah the son of Hacaliah. Now it happened in [b]the month Chislev, [c]*in* the twentieth year, while I was in [d]Susa the [1]capitol, [2] that [a]Hanani, one of my brothers, and [1]some men from Judah came; and I asked them concerning the Jews who had escaped *and* had survived the captivity, and about Jerusalem. [3] They said to me, "The remnant there in the [a]province who survived the captivity are in great distress and [b]reproach, and [b]the wall of Jerusalem is broken down and [c]its gates are burned with fire." **Neh. 1:4** When I heard these words, [a]I sat down and wept and mourned for days; and I was fasting and praying before [b]the God of heaven. [5] I said, "I beseech You, O LORD God of heaven, [a]the great and awesome God, [b]who preserves the covenant and lovingkindness for those who love Him and keep His commandments, [6] [a]let Your ear now be attentive and Your eyes open to hear the prayer of Your servant which I am praying before You now, day and night, on behalf of the sons of Israel Your servants, [b]confessing the sins of the sons of Israel which we have sinned against You; [a]I and my father's house have sinned. [7] "[a]We have acted very corruptly against You and have not kept the commandments, nor the statutes, nor the	¹ דִּבְרֵי נְחֶמְיָה בֶּן־חֲכַלְיָה וַיְהִי בְחֹדֶשׁ־כִּסְלֵו [כִּסְלֵיו] שְׁנַת עֶשְׂרִים וַאֲנִי הָיִיתִי בְּשׁוּשַׁן הַבִּירָה: ² וַיָּבֹא חֲנָנִי אֶחָד מֵאַחַי הוּא וַאֲנָשִׁים מִיהוּדָה וָאֶשְׁאָלֵם עַל־הַיְּהוּדִים הַפְּלֵיטָה אֲשֶׁר־נִשְׁאֲרוּ מִן־הַשֶּׁבִי וְעַל־יְרוּשָׁלִָם: ³ וַיֹּאמְרוּ לִי הַנִּשְׁאָרִים אֲשֶׁר־נִשְׁאֲרוּ מִן־הַשְּׁבִי שָׁם בַּמְּדִינָה בְּרָעָה גְדֹלָה וּבְחֶרְפָּה וְחוֹמַת יְרוּשָׁלִַם מְפֹרָצֶת וּשְׁעָרֶיהָ נִצְּתוּ בָאֵשׁ: ⁴ וַיְהִי כְּשָׁמְעִי אֶת־הַדְּבָרִים הָאֵלֶּה יָשַׁבְתִּי וָאֶבְכֶּה וָאֶתְאַבְּלָה יָמִים וָאֱהִי צָם וּמִתְפַּלֵּל לִפְנֵי אֱלֹהֵי הַשָּׁמָיִם: ⁵ וָאֹמַר אָנָּא יְהוָה אֱלֹהֵי הַשָּׁמַיִם הָאֵל הַגָּדוֹל וְהַנּוֹרָא שֹׁמֵר הַבְּרִית וָחֶסֶד לְאֹהֲבָיו וּלְשֹׁמְרֵי מִצְוֹתָיו: ⁶ תְּהִי נָא אָזְנְךָ־קַשֶּׁבֶת וְעֵינֶיךָ פְתֻוּחוֹת לִשְׁמֹעַ אֶל־תְּפִלַּת עַבְדְּךָ אֲשֶׁר אָנֹכִי מִתְפַּלֵּל לְפָנֶיךָ הַיּוֹם יוֹמָם וָלַיְלָה עַל־בְּנֵי יִשְׂרָאֵל עֲבָדֶיךָ וּמִתְוַדֶּה עַל־חַטֹּאות בְּנֵי־יִשְׂרָאֵל אֲשֶׁר חָטָאנוּ לָךְ וַאֲנִי וּבֵית־אָבִי חָטָאנוּ: ⁷ חֲבֹל חָבַלְנוּ

ordinances [b]which You commanded Your servant Moses. 8 "Remember the word which You commanded Your servant Moses, saying, 'If you are unfaithful I will scatter you among the peoples; 9 [a]but *if* you return to Me and keep My commandments and do them, though those of you who have been scattered were in the most remote part of the heavens, I [b]will gather them from there and will bring them [c]to the place where I have chosen to cause My name to dwell.' 10 "[a]They are Your servants and Your people whom You redeemed by Your great power and by Your strong hand. 11 "O Lord, I beseech You, [a]may Your ear be attentive to the prayer of Your servant and the prayer of Your servants who delight to [1]revere Your name, and make Your servant successful today and grant him compassion before this man."

Now I was the [b]cupbearer to the king.

לְךָ וְלֹא־שָׁמַרְנוּ אֶת־הַמִּצְוֹת וְאֶת־
הַחֻקִּים וְאֶת־הַמִּשְׁפָּטִים אֲשֶׁר צִוִּיתָ
אֶת־מֹשֶׁה עַבְדֶּךָ : 8 זְכָר־נָא אֶת־
הַדָּבָר אֲשֶׁר צִוִּיתָ אֶת־מֹשֶׁה עַבְדְּךָ
לֵאמֹר אַתֶּם תִּמְעָלוּ אֲנִי אָפִיץ
אֶתְכֶם בָּעַמִּים : 9 וְשַׁבְתֶּם אֵלַי
וּשְׁמַרְתֶּם מִצְוֹתַי וַעֲשִׂיתֶם אֹתָם
אִם־יִהְיֶה נִדַּחֲכֶם בִּקְצֵה הַשָּׁמַיִם
מִשָּׁם אֲקַבְּצֵם וַהֲבוֹאֹתִים
[וַהֲבִיאוֹתִים] אֶל־הַמָּקוֹם אֲשֶׁר
בָּחַרְתִּי לְשַׁכֵּן אֶת־שְׁמִי שָׁם : 10 וְהֵם
עֲבָדֶיךָ וְעַמֶּךָ אֲשֶׁר פָּדִיתָ בְּכֹחֲךָ
הַגָּדוֹל וּבְיָדְךָ הַחֲזָקָה : 11 אָנָּא
אֲדֹנָי תְּהִי נָא אָזְנְךָ־קַשֶּׁבֶת אֶל־
תְּפִלַּת עַבְדְּךָ וְאֶל־תְּפִלַּת עֲבָדֶיךָ
הַחֲפֵצִים לְיִרְאָה אֶת־שְׁמֶךָ
וְהַצְלִיחָה־נָּא לְעַבְדְּךָ הַיּוֹם וּתְנֵהוּ
לְרַחֲמִים לִפְנֵי הָאִישׁ הַזֶּה וַאֲנִי
הָיִיתִי מַשְׁקֶה לַמֶּלֶךְ : פ

References

Nehemiah 1:1
[1]Or *palace* or *citadel*
[a]Neh 10:1
[b]Zech 7:1
[c]Neh 2:1
[d]Esth 1:2; Dan 8:2

Nehemiah 1:2
[1]Lit *he and some*
[a]Neh 7:2

Nehemiah 1:3
[a]Neh 7:6
[b]Neh 2:17
[c]Neh 2:3

Nehemiah 1:4
[a]Ezra 9:3; 10:1
[b]Neh 2:4

Nehemiah 1:5
[a]Neh 4:14; 9:32; Dan 9:4
[b]Ex 20:6; Ps 89:2, 3

Nehemiah 1:6
[a]Dan 9:17
[b]Ezra 10:1; Dan 9:20
[c]2 Chr 29:6

Nehemiah 1:7
[a]Dan 9:5
[b]Deut 28:14

Nehemiah 1:8
[a]Lev 26:33

Nehemiah 1:9
[a]Deut 30:2, 3
[b]Deut 30:4
[c]Deut 12:5

Nehemiah 1:10
[a]Ex 32:11; Deut 9:29

Nehemiah 1:11
[1]Or *fear*

Process of Discovery

Linguistics Section

Linguistic Structure

[Introduction] 1 The words of *°*Nehemiah the son of Hacaliah. Now it happened in *°*the month Chislev, *°in* the twentieth year, while I was in *°*Susa the [1]capitol, **2** that *°*Hanani , one of my brothers, and [1]some men from Judah came;

[Nehemiah's Question] and I asked them concerning the Jews who had escaped *and* had survived the captivity, and about Jerusalem.

[Answer to the question] **3** They said to me, "The remnant there in the *°*province who survived the captivity are in great distress and *°*reproach, and *°*the wall of Jerusalem is broken down and *°*its gates are burned with fire."

[Nehemiah's Prayer] **4** When I heard these words, *°*I sat down and wept and mourned for days; and I was fasting and praying before *°*the God of heaven. **5** I said, "I beseech You, O LORD God of heaven, *°*the great and awesome God, *°*who preserves the covenant and lovingkindness for those who love Him and keep His commandments, **6** *°*let Your ear now be attentive and Your eyes open to hear the prayer of Your servant which I am praying before You now, day and night, on behalf of the sons of Israel Your servants, *°*confessing the sins of the sons of Israel which we have sinned against You; *°*I and my father's house have sinned. **7** "*°*We have acted very corruptly against You and have not kept the commandments, nor the statutes, nor the ordinances *°*which You commanded Your servant Moses. **8** "Remember the word which You commanded Your servant Moses, saying, '*°*If you are unfaithful I will scatter you among the peoples; **9** *°*but *if* you return to Me and keep My commandments and do them, though those of you who have been scattered were in the most remote part of the heavens, I *°*will gather them from there and will bring them *°*to the place where I have chosen to cause My name to dwell.' **10** "'*°*They are Your servants and Your people whom You redeemed by Your great power and by Your strong hand. **11** "O Lord, I beseech You, *°*may Your ear be attentive to the prayer of Your servant and the prayer of Your servants who delight to [1]revere Your name, and make Your servant successful today and grant him compassion before this man."

[Nehemiah's position in the Persian Government] Now I was the *°*cupbearer to the king.

Discussion

The introduction to this book says that Nehemiah was in Susa, the Persian Empire's capital. He wanted to know what was happening with the group of Jews who returned to Jerusalem from Susa. After hearing the news, Nehemiah offered a prayer to the LORD.

Questioning the Passage

1. What is the twentieth year? (v. 1)

   This year was the twentieth year of the reign of the Persian King Darius, son of Ahasuerus and Queen Esther. In that year, Nehemiah learned that the rebuilding of the walls of Jerusalem had not happened.

2. Who were the people who escaped captivity? (v. 2)

   When the Babylonians took the Hebrew people into captivity and exiled them from Judah, they only took approximately fifteen percent of the population. The Babylonians took the royalty, nobility, and highly educated people into Exile. The peasants were left in the land to fend for themselves.

Biblical Personalities

1. "Hachaliah or Hacaliah (חֲכַלְיָה in the Hebrew) was the father of Nehemiah, the author of the Book of Nehemiah, which is a book of the Hebrew Bible, known to Jews as the Tanakh and to Christians as the Old Testament. Hachaliah's name is mentioned at the beginning of the book and in Nehemiah 10:1: the references to Hachaliah distinguish Nehemiah from

others with the same name. Little is known about his status: Bowman notes that many attempts have been made to explain the name Hacaliah, "but none is persuasive".[5]

2. Hanani – "Probably a brother of Nehemiah (Nehemiah 1:2 ; 7:2), who reported to him the melancholy condition of Jerusalem. Nehemiah afterwards appointed him to have charge of the city gates."[6]

3. "Moses, Hebrew Moshe, (flourished 14th–13th century BCE), Hebrew prophet, teacher, and leader who, in the 13th century BCE (before the Common Era, or BC), delivered his people from Egyptian slavery. In the Covenant ceremony at Mt. Sinai, where the Ten Commandments were promulgated, he founded the religious community known as Israel. As the interpreter of these Covenant stipulations, he was the organizer of the community's religious and civil traditions. In the Judaic tradition, he is revered as the greatest prophet and teacher, and Judaism has sometimes loosely been called Mosaism, or the Mosaic faith, in Western Christendom. His influence continues to be felt in the religious life, moral concerns, and social ethics of Western civilization, and therein lies his undying significance."[7]

---

[5] "Hachaliah," Wikipedia (Wikimedia Foundation, September 12, 2020), https://en.wikipedia.org/wiki/Hachaliah.

[6] "Hanani Definition and Meaning - Bible Dictionary." biblestudytools.com. Accessed April 22, 2021. https://www.biblestudytools.com/dictionary/hanani/.

[7] https://www.britannica.com/biography/Moses-Hebrew-prophet

Biblical Locations

1. "Susa (/ˈsuːsə/; Cuneiform:*šušin*[ki]; Persian: شوش *Šuš* [ʃuʃ]; Hebrew: שׁוּשָׁן *Šušān*; Greek: Σοῦσα [ˈsuːsa]; Syriac: ܫܘܫ *Šuš*;[1] Middle Persian) was an ancient city in the lower Zagros Mountains about 250 km (160 mi) east of the Tigris, between the Karkheh and Dez Rivers. One of the most important cities of the Ancient Near East, Susa served as the capital of Elam and the Achaemenid Empire, and remained a strategic centre during the Parthian and Sasanian periods. The site currently consists of three archaeological mounds, covering an area of around one square kilometre.[2] The modern Iranian town of Shush is located on the site of ancient Susa. Shush is identified as Shushan, mentioned in the Book of Esther and other Biblical books."[8]

2. "Judah, one of the 12 tribes of Israel, descended from Judah, who was the fourth son born to Jacob and his first wife, Leah. It is disputed whether the name Judah was originally that of the tribe or the territory it occupied and which was transposed from which."[9]

Thoughts

The pattern of Nehemiah's prayer should be familiar to Christians. It is a prayer of confession. Nehemiah notes that the people did not follow the Torah as they should have. He spoke about the covenant that the LORD had with the people of Israel. The

---

[8] "Susa," Wikipedia (Wikimedia Foundation, April 19, 2021), https://en.wikipedia.org/wiki/Susa.
[9] "Judah," Encyclopædia Britannica (Encyclopædia Britannica, inc.), accessed April 22, 2021, https://www.britannica.com/topic/Judah-Hebrew-tribe.

people had broken the covenant by not following the word of the LORD. Nehemiah felt that enough time had passed and that the LORD's anger against Israel would be gone. Nehemiah probably knew the words of Jeremiah in which Jeremiah told the people that the Exile would last seventy years. That period was over.

Chapter Two

Language

New American Standard 1995	**Hebrew**
Neh. 2:1 And it came about in the month Nisan, [a]in the twentieth year of King [b]Artaxerxes, that wine *was* before him, and [c]I took up the wine and gave it to the king. Now I had not been sad in his presence. [2] So the king said to me, "Why is your face sad though you are not sick? [a]This is nothing but sadness of heart." Then I was very much afraid. [3] I said to the king, "[a]Let the king live forever. Why should my face not be sad [b]when the city, the place of my fathers' tombs, lies desolate and its gates have been consumed by fire?" [4] Then the king said to me, "What would you request?" [a]So I prayed to the God of heaven. [5] I said to the king, "If it please the king, and if your servant has found favor before you, send me to Judah, to the city of my fathers' tombs, that I may rebuild it." [6] Then the king said to me, the queen sitting beside him, "How long will your journey be, and when will you return?" So it pleased the king to send me, and [a]I gave him a definite time. [7] And I said to the king, "If it please the king, let letters be given me [a]for the governors *of the provinces* beyond the River, that they may allow me to pass through until I come to Judah, [8] and a letter to Asaph the keeper of the king's [a]forest, that he may give me timber to make beams for the gates of [b]the fortress which is by the [1]temple, for the wall of the	Neh. 2:1 וַיְהִ֣י ׀ בְּחֹ֣דֶשׁ נִיסָ֗ן שְׁנַ֥ת עֶשְׂרִ֛ים לְאַרְתַּחְשַׁ֥סְתְּא הַמֶּ֖לֶךְ יַ֣יִן לְפָנָ֑יו וָאֶשָּׂ֤א אֶת־הַיַּ֨יִן֙ וָאֶתְּנָ֣ה לַמֶּ֔לֶךְ וְלֹא־הָיִ֥יתִי רַ֖ע לְפָנָֽיו ׃ [2] וַיֹּאמֶר֩ לִ֨י הַמֶּ֜לֶךְ מַדּ֣וּעַ ׀ פָּנֶ֣יךָ רָעִ֗ים וְאַתָּה֙ אֵֽינְךָ֣ חוֹלֶ֔ה אֵ֥ין זֶ֛ה כִּי־אִ֖ם רֹ֣עַֽ לֵ֑ב וָאִירָ֖א הַרְבֵּ֥ה מְאֹֽד ׃ [3] וָאֹמַ֣ר לַמֶּ֔לֶךְ הַמֶּ֖לֶךְ לְעוֹלָ֣ם יִחְיֶ֑ה מַדּ֜וּעַ לֹא־יֵרְע֣וּ פָנַ֗י אֲשֶׁ֨ר הָעִ֜יר בֵּית־קִבְר֤וֹת אֲבֹתַי֙ חֲרֵבָ֔ה וּשְׁעָרֶ֖יהָ אֻכְּל֥וּ בָאֵֽשׁ ׃ ס [4] וַיֹּ֤אמֶר לִי֙ הַמֶּ֔לֶךְ עַל־מַה־זֶּ֖ה אַתָּ֣ה מְבַקֵּ֑שׁ וָֽאֶתְפַּלֵּ֔ל אֶל־אֱלֹהֵ֖י הַשָּׁמָֽיִם ׃ [5] וָאֹמַ֣ר לַמֶּ֔לֶךְ אִם־עַל־ הַמֶּ֣לֶךְ ט֔וֹב וְאִם־יִיטַ֥ב עַבְדְּךָ֖ לְפָנֶ֑יךָ אֲשֶׁ֧ר תִּשְׁלָחֵ֣נִי אֶל־יְהוּדָ֗ה אֶל־עִ֛יר קִבְר֥וֹת אֲבֹתַ֖י וְאֶבְנֶֽנָּה ׃ [6] וַיֹּאמֶר֩ לִ֨י הַמֶּ֜לֶךְ וְהַשֵּׁגַ֣ל ׀ יוֹשֶׁ֣בֶת אֶצְל֗וֹ עַד־מָתַ֛י יִהְיֶ֥ה מַֽהֲלָכְךָ֖ וּמָתַ֣י תָּשׁ֑וּב וַיִּיטַ֤ב לִפְנֵֽי־הַמֶּ֨לֶךְ֙ וַיִּשְׁלָחֵ֔נִי וָאֶתְּנָ֥ה ל֖וֹ זְמָֽן ׃ [7] וָאוֹמַר֮ לַמֶּלֶךְ֒ אִם־עַל־הַמֶּ֣לֶךְ ט֔וֹב אִגְּר֖וֹת יִתְּנוּ־ לִ֔י עַל־פַּחֲו֖וֹת עֵ֣בֶר הַנָּהָ֑ר אֲשֶׁר֙

city and for the house to which I will go." And the king granted *them* to me because *c*the good hand of my God *was* on me.

Neh. 2:9 Then I came to *a*the governors *of the provinces* beyond the River and gave them the king's letters. Now *b*the king had sent with me officers of the army and horsemen. **10** When *a*Sanballat the Horonite and Tobiah the Ammonite [1]official heard *about it,* it was very displeasing to them that someone had come to seek the welfare of the sons of Israel.

Neh. 2:11 So I *a*came to Jerusalem and was there three days. **12** And I arose in the night, I and a few men with me. I did not tell anyone what my God was putting into my [1]mind to do for Jerusalem and there was no animal with me except the animal on which I was riding. **13** So I went out at night by *a*the Valley Gate in the direction of the Dragon's Well and *on* to the [1]Refuse Gate, inspecting the walls of Jerusalem *b*which were broken down and its *c*gates which were consumed by fire. **14** Then I passed on to *a*the Fountain Gate and *b*the King's Pool, but there was no place for [1]my mount to pass. **15** So I went up at night by the *a*ravine and inspected the wall. Then I entered the Valley Gate again and returned. **16** The officials did not know where I had gone or what I had done; nor had I as yet told the Jews, the priests, the nobles, the officials or the rest who did the work.

Neh. 2:17 Then I said to them, "You see the bad situation we are in, that *a*Jerusalem is desolate and its gates burned

יַעֲבִירוּנִי עַד אֲשֶׁר־אָבוֹא אֶל־
יְהוּדָה ׃ ⁸ וָאֶוֹבֶרת אֶל־אָסָף שֹׁמֵר
הַפַּרְדֵּס אֲשֶׁר לַמֶּלֶךְ אֲשֶׁר יִתֶּן־לִי
עֵצִים לְקָרוֹת אֶת־שַׁעֲרֵי הַבִּירָה
אֲשֶׁר־לַבַּיִת וּלְחוֹמַת הָעִיר וְלַבַּיִת
אֲשֶׁר־אָבוֹא אֵלָיו וַיִּתֶּן־לִי הַמֶּלֶךְ
כְּיַד־אֱלֹהַי הַטּוֹבָה עָלָי ׃ ⁹ וָאָבוֹא
אֶל־פַּחֲווֹת עֵבֶר הַנָּהָר וָאֶתְּנָה
לָהֶם אֵת אִגְּרוֹת הַמֶּלֶךְ וַיִּשְׁלַח
עִמִּי הַמֶּלֶךְ שָׂרֵי חַיִל וּפָרָשִׁים ׃ ⁱ⁰ פ
וַיִּשְׁמַע סַנְבַלַּט הַחֹרֹנִי וְטוֹבִיָּה
הָעֶבֶד הָעַמֹּנִי וַיֵּרַע לָהֶם רָעָה
גְדֹלָה אֲשֶׁר־בָּא אָדָם לְבַקֵּשׁ טוֹבָה
לִבְנֵי יִשְׂרָאֵל ׃ ¹¹ וָאָבוֹא אֶל־
יְרוּשָׁלִַם וָאֱהִי־שָׁם יָמִים שְׁלֹשָׁה ׃ ¹²
וָאָקוּם ׀ לַיְלָה אֲנִי וַאֲנָשִׁים ׀ מְעַט
עִמִּי וְלֹא־הִגַּדְתִּי לְאָדָם מָה אֱלֹהַי
נֹתֵן אֶל־לִבִּי לַעֲשׂוֹת לִירוּשָׁלִָם
וּבְהֵמָה אֵין עִמִּי כִּי אִם־הַבְּהֵמָה
אֲשֶׁר אֲנִי רֹכֵב בָּהּ ׃ ¹³ וָאֵצְאָה
בְשַׁעַר־הַגַּיְא לַיְלָה וְאֶל־פְּנֵי עֵין
הַתַּנִּין וְאֶל־שַׁעַר הָאַשְׁפֹּת וָאֱהִי
שֹׂבֵר בְּחוֹמֹת יְרוּשָׁלִַם אֲשֶׁר־
[הֵם ׀] הַמְפֹרוָצִים [פְּרוּצִים]
וּשְׁעָרֶיהָ אֻכְּלוּ בָאֵשׁ ׃ ¹⁴ וָאֶעֱבֹר
אֶל־שַׁעַר הָעַיִן וְאֶל־בְּרֵכַת הַמֶּלֶךְ
וְאֵין־מָקוֹם לַבְּהֵמָה לַעֲבֹר תַּחְתָּי ׃
¹⁵ וָאֱהִי עֹלֶה בַנַּחַל לַיְלָה וָאֱהִי

by fire. Come, let us rebuild the wall of Jerusalem so that we will no longer be a reproach." **18** I told them how the hand of my God had been favorable to me and also about the king's words which he had spoken to me. Then they said, "Let us arise and build." [a]So they put their hands to the good *work*. **19** But when Sanballat the Horonite and Tobiah the Ammonite [1]official, and [a]Geshem the Arab heard *it*, [b]they mocked us and despised us and said, "What is this thing you are doing? [a]Are you rebelling against the king?" **20** So I answered them and said to them, "[a]The God of heaven will give us success; therefore we His servants will arise and build, [b]but you have no portion, right or memorial in Jerusalem."

שָׁבֵר בַּחוֹמָה וָאָשׁוּב וָאָבוֹא בְּשַׁעַר
הַגַּיְא וָאָשׁוּב׃ 16 וְהַסְּגָנִים לֹא יָדְעוּ
אָנָה הָלַכְתִּי וּמָה אֲנִי עֹשֶׂה
וְלַיְּהוּדִים וְלַכֹּהֲנִים וְלַחֹרִים
וְלַסְּגָנִים וּלְיֶתֶר עֹשֵׂה הַמְּלָאכָה
עַד־כֵּן לֹא הִגַּדְתִּי׃ 17 וָאוֹמַר
אֲלֵהֶם אַתֶּם רֹאִים הָרָעָה אֲשֶׁר
אֲנַחְנוּ בָהּ אֲשֶׁר יְרוּשָׁלַם חֲרֵבָה
וּשְׁעָרֶיהָ נִצְּתוּ בָאֵשׁ לְכוּ וְנִבְנֶה
אֶת־חוֹמַת יְרוּשָׁלַם וְלֹא־נִהְיֶה עוֹד
חֶרְפָּה׃ 18 וָאַגִּיד לָהֶם אֶת־יַד
אֱלֹהַי אֲשֶׁר־הִיא טוֹבָה עָלַי וְאַף־
דִּבְרֵי הַמֶּלֶךְ אֲשֶׁר אָמַר־לִי
וַיֹּאמְרוּ נָקוּם וּבָנִינוּ וַיְחַזְּקוּ יְדֵיהֶם
לַטּוֹבָה׃ פ 19 וַיִּשְׁמַע סַנְבַלַּט
הַחֹרֹנִי וְטֹבִיָּה הָעֶבֶד הָעַמּוֹנִי
וְגֶשֶׁם הָעַרְבִי וַיַּלְעִגוּ לָנוּ וַיִּבְזוּ
עָלֵינוּ וַיֹּאמְרוּ מָה־הַדָּבָר הַזֶּה
אֲשֶׁר אַתֶּם עֹשִׂים הַעַל הַמֶּלֶךְ אַתֶּם
מֹרְדִים׃ 20 וָאָשִׁיב אוֹתָם דָּבָר
וָאוֹמַר לָהֶם אֱלֹהֵי הַשָּׁמַיִם הוּא
יַצְלִיחַ לָנוּ וַאֲנַחְנוּ עֲבָדָיו נָקוּם
וּבָנִינוּ וְלָכֶם אֵין־חֵלֶק וּצְדָקָה
וְזִכָּרוֹן בִּירוּשָׁלָם׃

References

Nehemiah 2:1
*a*Neh 1:1
*b*Ezra 7:1
*c*Neh 1:11

Nehemiah 2:2
*a*Prov 15:13

Nehemiah 2:3
*a*Dan 2:4
*b*2 Kin 25:8-10; 2 Chr 36:19; Neh 1:3; Jer 52:12-14

Nehemiah 2:4
*a*Neh 1:4

Nehemiah 2:6
*a*Neh 13:6

Nehemiah 2:7
*a*Ezra 7:21; 8:36

Nehemiah 2:8
*1*Lit *house*
*a*Eccl 2:5, 6
*b*Neh 7:2
*c*Ezra 7:6; Neh 2:18

Nehemiah 2:9
*a*Neh 2:7
*b*Ezra 8:22

Nehemiah 2:10
*1*Lit *servant*
*a*Neh 2:19; 4:1

Nehemiah 2:11
*a*Ezra 8:32

Nehemiah 2:12
*1*Lit *heart*

Nehemiah 2:13
*1*Lit *Gate of Ash-heaps*
*a*Neh 3:13
*b*Neh 1:3
*c*Neh 2:3, 17

Nehemiah 2:14
*1*Lit *the animal under me*
*a*Neh 3:15
*b*2 Kin 20:20

Nehemiah 2:15
*a*John 18:1

Nehemiah 2:17
*a*Neh 1:3

Nehemiah 2:18
*a*2 Sam 2:7

Nehemiah 2:19
*1*Lit *servant*
*a*Neh 6:6
*b*Neh 4:1

Nehemiah 2:20
*a*Ezra 4:3
*b*Neh 2:4; Acts 8:21

Process of Discovery

Linguistics Section

Linguistic Structure

[Introduction] [1]   And it came about in the month Nisan, *[a]*in the twentieth year of King *[b]*Artaxerxes, that wine *was* before him, and *[I* took up the wine and gave it to the king. Now I had not been sad in his presence.

A [King's question] [2] So the king said to me, "Why is your face sad though you are not sick? *[a]*This is nothing but sadness of heart."

> **A' [Nehemiah's response]** Then I was very much afraid. [3] I said to the king, "*[a]*Let the king live forever. Why should my face not be sad *[b]*when the city, the place of my fathers' tombs, lies desolate and its gates have been consumed by fire?"

A1 [King's Question] [4] Then the king said to me, "What would you request?"

> **A1' [Nehemiah's Response]** *[a]*So I prayed to the God of heaven. [5] I said to the king, "If it please the king, and if your servant has found favor before you, send me to Judah, to the city of my fathers' tombs, that I may rebuild it."

A2 [King's Question] [6] Then the king said to me, the queen sitting beside him, "How long will your journey be, and when will you return?"

> **A2' [Nehemiah's Response]** So it pleased the king to send me, and *[I* gave him a definite time. [7] And I said to the king, "If it please the king, let letters be given me *[a]*for the governors *of the provinces* beyond the River, that they may allow me to pass through until I come to Judah, [8] and a letter to Asaph the keeper of the king's *[a]*forest, that he may give me timber to make beams for the gates of *[b]*the fortress which is by the *[1]*temple, for the wall of the city and for the house to which I will go." And the king granted *them* to me because *[c]*the good hand of my God *was* on me.

[Nehemiah prepares to leave] [9]   Then I came to *[a]*the governors *of the provinces* beyond the River and gave them the king's letters. Now *[b]*the king had sent with me officers of the army and horsemen. [10] When *[a]*Sanballat the Horonite and Tobiah the Ammonite *[1]*official heard *about it,* it was very displeasing to them that someone had come to seek the welfare of the sons of Israel.

[Nehemiah's arrival] [11] So I *came to Jerusalem and was there three days. [12] And I arose in the night, I and a few men with me. I did not tell anyone what my God was putting into my [1]mind to do for Jerusalem and there was no animal with me except the animal on which I was riding. [13] So I went out at night by *the Valley Gate in the direction of the Dragon's Well and *on* to the [1]Refuse Gate, inspecting the walls of Jerusalem *which were broken down and its *gates which were consumed by fire. [14] Then I passed on to *the Fountain Gate and *the King's Pool, but there was no place for [1]my mount to pass. [15] So I went up at night by the *ravine and inspected the wall. Then I entered the Valley Gate again and returned.

[Nehemiah approved the offiials] [16] The officials did not know where I had gone or what I had done; nor had I as yet told the Jews, the priests, the nobles, the officials or the rest who did the work. [17] Then I said to them, "You see the bad situation we are in, that *Jerusalem is desolate and its gates burned by fire. Come, let us rebuild the wall of Jerusalem so that we will no longer be a reproach." [18] I told them how the hand of my God had been favorable to me and also about the king's words which he had spoken to me.

[The officials response] Then they said, "Let us arise and build." *So they put their hands to the good *work*.

[The resistence] [19] But when Sanballat the Horonite and Tobiah the Ammonite [1]official, and *Geshem the Arab heard *it,* *they mocked us and despised us and said, "What is this thing you are doing? *Are you rebelling against the king?" [20] So I answered them and said to them, "*The God of heaven will give us success; therefore we His servants will arise and build, *but you have no portion, right or memorial in Jerusalem."

Discussion

Three questions/answers sections form a very simplistic chiasm at the beginning of the chapter. The chapter is concerned with Nehemiah going to Jerusalem to help get the walls around the city rebuilt. The end of the chapter refers to the persons who did not want the work to commence.

Questioning the Passage

1. Is there a significance to the month of Nisan? (v. 1)

   The month of Nisan may be when the actual event occurred. It could be symbolic because Nisan is the month of the Passover. The Jews of Persia would have celebrated their freedom from the slavery imposed upon them by the Egyptians. It is a month of salvation. The rebuilding of Jerusalem and the Temple would fortify the LORD's salvation to His people because the Exile would be officially and religiously over.

2. What was Nehemiah's response to the King's question in verse four? Nehemiah offered a prayer to the LORD, which is not recorded before answering the King's question.[10]

3. Is there a significance to Nehemiah being in Jerusalem for three days before getting the work started? (v. 11)

   The number three is symbolic of the work of the LORD. Nehemiah was ready to start the LORD's work. The LORD determined after seventy years of Exile that His people must return to Jerusalem to rebuild the city and the Temple. The number three indicates that the rebuilding of Jerusalem was a divinely inspired event.

Personalities

1. Asaph was the keeper of the King's forest.

---

[10] Nosson Scherman and Meir Zlotowitz, *The Writings = Kesuvim / The Writings: with a Commentary Anthologized from Rabbinic Writings = Ketuvim: 'im Perush Rashi, Metsudat David, Metsudat Tsiyon, ye-'od* (Brooklyn, NY: Mesorah Publications, 2016).

2. *"Sanballat the Horonite.* Sanballat was probably from a town named Horonaim in Moab and thus most likely was a Moabite. Tobiah was an Ammonite and Geshem an Arab. All three peoples were leaders of anti-Jewish regions and peoples adjacent to Judah and Jerusalem, fearful of the growing influence of the Jews."[11]

3. Tobia – "Wealthy governor of Ammon with strong Judaean connections; opposed Nehemiah's rebuilding of Jerusalem's wall during the fifth century BC."[12]

4. Geshem the Arab – "Geshem the Arabian (or Geshem the Arab; Hebrew: גֶשֶׁם הָעַרְבִי) is the only Arab person mentioned in the Hebrew Bible.[1] He was an ally of Sanballat and Tobiah and adversary of Nehemiah (Neh. 2:19, 6:1). In Neh. 6:6 he is called "Gashmu," which is probably more correct, as an Arab tribe named "Gushamu" is known (Cook, "Aramaic Glossary," s.v. גשמו). When Nehemiah proceeded to rebuild the walls of Jerusalem, the Samaritans and the Arabs made efforts to hinder him. Geshem or Gashmu, who probably was the chief of the Arabs, joined the Samaritans and accused Nehemiah of conspiracy against the Persian king." "Geshem the Arabian," Wikipedia (Wikimedia Foundation, November 14, 2020), https://en.wikipedia.org/wiki/Geshem_the_Arabian.

5. Ammonites – "The Ammonites were a pagan people who worshiped the gods Milcom and Molech. God commanded the Israelites not to marry these pagans, because intermarriage would lead the Israelites to worship

---

[11] The Institute for Creation Research, accessed April 22, 2021, https://www.icr.org/books/defenders/2489/.
[12] Logos Bible Software, "Tobiah (Ammonite)," Biblia, accessed April 22, 2021, https://biblia.com/factbook/Tobiah-(Ammonite).

false gods. Solomon disobeyed and married Naamah the Ammonite (1 Kings 14:21), and, as God had warned, he was drawn into idolatry (1 Kings 11:1-8). Molech was a fire-god with the face of a calf; his images had arms outstretched to receive the babies who were sacrificed to him. Like their god, the Ammonites were cruel. When Nahash the Ammonite was asked for terms of a treaty (1 Samuel 11:2), he proposed gouging out the right eye of each Israelite man. Amos 1:13 says that the Ammonites would rip open pregnant women in the territories they conquered."[13]

[13] GotQuestions.org, "Home," GotQuestions.org, August 14, 2007, https://www.gotquestions.org/Ammonites.html.

Biblical Locations

1. Jerusalem

   The following map is a more modern rendition of the city. However, it does

   show where the gates of the city were located.

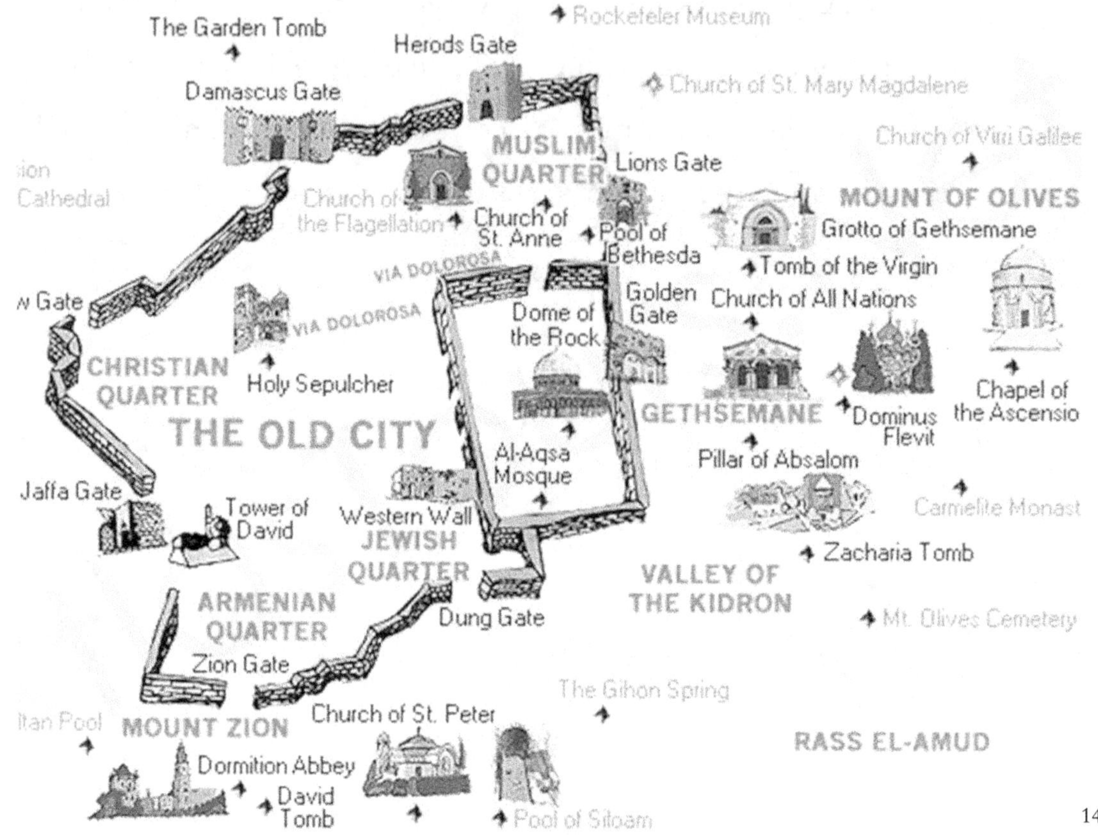

Culture Section

Discussion

Persian Kings lived in isolation. The monarch was considered sacred. Besides, the

monarchs were paranoid that they would be murdered at any time. The queen and

his children could not approach the King without explicit orders. The King had

many enemies due to his army's conquests. The people were jealous of the king

---

[14] https://i.pinimg.com/originals/cc/31/b2/cc31b20a0edafa36b3079c0b274579df.jpg

because he lived in lavish abundance. Cupbearers were carefully selected from persons that the King had complete trust in. Most of the time, family members could not become cupbearers. Poison in wine was a common way in the Near East to assassinate a noble or royal person. Therefore, the cupbearer became the most trusted person in the kingdom.

Thoughts

Nehemiah was on a mission from the LORD. He was willing to give up his lucrative position as the first in command to the King. Rebuilding the city of the LORD and His Temple was more important to him. Would you be willing to make a similar sacrifice to the LORD if He called you?

Chapter Three

Language

New American Standard 1995	Hebrew
Neh. 3:1 Then *ᵃ*Eliashib the high priest arose with his brothers the priests and built *ᵇ*the Sheep Gate; they consecrated it and *ᶜ*hung its doors. They consecrated ¹the wall to *ᵈ*the Tower of the Hundred *and* *ᵉ*the Tower of Hananel. ² Next to him *ᵃ*the men of Jericho built, and next to ¹them Zaccur the son of Imri built. **Neh. 3:3** Now the sons of Hassenaah built *ᵃ*the Fish Gate; they laid its beams and hung its doors with its bolts and bars. ⁴ Next to them Meremoth the son of Uriah the son of Hakkoz made repairs. And next to him Meshullam the son of Berechiah the son of Meshezabel made repairs. And next to ¹him Zadok the son of Baana *also* made repairs. ⁵ Moreover, next to ¹him the Tekoites made repairs, but their nobles did not ²support the work of their masters. **Neh. 3:6** Joiada the son of Paseah and Meshullam the son of Besodeiah repaired *ᵃ*the Old Gate; they laid its beams and hung its doors with its bolts and its bars. ⁷ Next to them Melatiah the Gibeonite and Jadon the Meronothite, the men of Gibeon and of Mizpah, ¹also made repairs for the official seat of the *ᵃ*governor *of the province* beyond the River. ⁸ Next to him Uzziel the son of Harhaiah of the *ᵃ*goldsmiths made repairs. And next to him Hananiah, one of the perfumers, made repairs, and they restored Jerusalem as far as *ᵇ*the Broad Wall. ⁹ Next to them	1 וַיָּ֡קָם אֶלְיָשִׁיב֩ הַכֹּהֵ֨ן הַגָּד֜וֹל וְאֶחָ֣יו הַכֹּהֲנִים֮ וַיִּבְנוּ֮ אֶת־שַׁ֣עַר הַצֹּאן֒ הֵ֣מָּה קִדְּשׁ֔וּהוּ וַֽיַּעֲמִ֖ידוּ דַּלְתֹתָ֑יו וְעַד־מִגְדַּ֤ל הַמֵּאָה֙ קִדְּשׁ֔וּהוּ עַ֖ד מִגְדַּ֥ל חֲנַנְאֵֽל׃ ס 2 וְעַל־יָד֥וֹ בָנ֖וּ אַנְשֵׁ֣י יְרֵח֑וֹ ס וְעַל־יָד֣וֹ בָנָ֔ה זַכּ֖וּר בֶּן־אִמְרִֽי׃ ס 3 וְאֵת֙ שַׁ֣עַר הַדָּגִ֔ים בָּנ֖וּ בְּנֵ֣י הַסְּנָאָ֑ה הֵ֣מָּה קֵר֔וּהוּ וַֽיַּעֲמִ֙ידוּ֙ דַּלְתֹתָ֔יו מַנְעוּלָ֖יו וּבְרִיחָֽיו׃ ס 4 וְעַל־יָדָ֣ם הֶחֱזִ֗יק מְרֵמ֤וֹת בֶּן־אוּרִיָּה֙ בֶּן־הַקּ֔וֹץ ס וְעַל־יָדָ֣ם הֶחֱזִ֔יק מְשֻׁלָּ֖ם בֶּן־בֶּֽרֶכְיָ֑ה בֶּן־מְשֵׁיזַבְאֵ֑ל ס וְעַל־יָדָ֣ם הֶחֱזִ֔יק צָד֖וֹק בֶּן־בַּעֲנָֽא׃ ס 5 וְעַל־יָדָ֖ם הֶחֱזִ֣יקוּ הַתְּקוֹעִ֑ים וְאַדִּֽירֵיהֶם֙ לֹא־הֵבִ֣יאוּ צַוָּרָ֔ם בַּעֲבֹדַ֖ת אֲדֹנֵיהֶֽם׃ ס 6 וְאֵת֩ שַׁ֨עַר הַיְשָׁנָ֜ה הֶחֱזִ֗יקוּ יֽוֹיָדָע֙ בֶּן־פָּסֵ֔חַ וּמְשֻׁלָּ֖ם בֶּן־בְּסֽוֹדְיָ֑ה הֵ֣מָּה קֵר֔וּהוּ וַֽיַּעֲמִ֙ידוּ֙ דַּלְתֹתָ֔יו וּמַנְעֻלָ֖יו וּבְרִיחָֽיו׃ ס 7 וְעַל־יָדָ֣ם הֶחֱזִ֗יק מְלַטְיָ֣ה הַגִּבְעֹנִ֗י וְיָדוֹן֙ הַמֵּרֹ֣נֹתִ֔י אַנְשֵׁ֥י גִבְע֖וֹן וְהַמִּצְפָּ֑ה לְכִסֵּ֕א פַּחַ֖ת עֵ֥בֶר הַנָּהָֽר׃ ס 8 עַ֣ל יָד֞וֹ הֶחֱזִ֗יק עֻזִּיאֵ֤ל בֶּֽן־חַרְהֲיָה֙ צֽוֹרְפִ֔ים ס וְעַל־

Rephaiah the son of Hur, ^athe official of half the district of Jerusalem, made repairs. **10** Next to them Jedaiah the son of Harumaph made repairs opposite his house. And next to him Hattush the son of Hashabneiah made repairs. **11** Malchijah the son of Harim and Hasshub the son of Pahath-moab repaired another section and ^athe Tower of Furnaces. **12** Next to him Shallum the son of Hallohesh, ^athe official of half the district of Jerusalem, made repairs, he and his daughters.

Neh. 3:13 Hanun and the inhabitants of Zanoah repaired ^athe Valley Gate. They built it and hung its doors with its bolts and its bars, and a thousand cubits of the wall to the [1]Refuse Gate.

Neh. 3:14 Malchijah the son of Rechab, the official of the district of ^aBeth-haccherem repaired the [1b]Refuse Gate. He built it and hung its doors with its bolts and its bars.

Neh. 3:15 Shallum the son of Col-hozeh, the official of the district of Mizpah, ^arepaired the Fountain Gate. He built it, covered it and hung its doors with its bolts and its bars, and the wall of the Pool of Shelah at ^bthe king's garden as far as ^cthe steps that descend from the city of David. **16** After him Nehemiah the son of Azbuk, ^aofficial of half the district of Beth-zur, made repairs as far as *a point* opposite the tombs of David, and as far as ^bthe artificial pool and the house of the mighty men. **17** After him the Levites carried out repairs *under* Rehum the son of Bani. Next to him Hashabiah, the

יָדוֹ הֶחֱזִיק חֲנַנְיָה בֶּן־הָרַקָּחִים

וַיַּעַזְבוּ יְרוּשָׁלַם עַד הַחוֹמָה

הָרְחָבָה : ס וְעַל־יָדָם הֶחֱזִיק ⁹

רְפָיָה בֶן־חוּר שַׂר חֲצִי פֶּלֶךְ

יְרוּשָׁלָם : ס וְעַל־יָדָם הֶחֱזִיק ¹⁰

יְדָיָה בֶּן־חֲרוּמַף וְנֶגֶד בֵּיתוֹ ס

וְעַל־יָדוֹ הֶחֱזִיק חַטּוּשׁ בֶּן־

חֲשַׁבְנְיָה : מִדָּה שֵׁנִית הֶחֱזִיק ¹¹

מַלְכִּיָה בֶן־חָרִם וְחַשּׁוּב בֶּן־פַּחַת

מוֹאָב וְאֵת מִגְדַּל הַתַּנּוּרִים : ס ¹²

וְעַל־יָדוֹ הֶחֱזִיק שַׁלּוּם בֶּן־הַלּוֹחֵשׁ

שַׂר חֲצִי פֶּלֶךְ יְרוּשָׁלָם הוּא

וּבְנוֹתָיו : ס אֵת שַׁעַר הַגַּיְא ¹³

הֶחֱזִיק חָנוּן וְיֹשְׁבֵי זָנוֹחַ הֵמָּה

בָנוּהוּ וַיַּעֲמִידוּ דַּלְתֹתָיו מַנְעֻלָיו

וּבְרִיחָיו וְאֶלֶף אַמָּה בַּחוֹמָה עַד

שַׁעַר הָשְׁפוֹת : וְאֵת שַׁעַר ¹⁴

הָאַשְׁפּוֹת הֶחֱזִיק מַלְכִּיָּה בֶּן־רֵכָב

שַׂר פֶּלֶךְ בֵּית־הַכָּרֶם הוּא יִבְנֶנּוּ

וְיַעֲמִיד דַּלְתֹתָיו מַנְעֻלָיו וּבְרִיחָיו :

ס וְאֵת שַׁעַר הָעַיִן הֶחֱזִיק שַׁלּוּן ¹⁵

בֶּן־כָּל־חֹזֶה שַׂר פֶּלֶךְ הַמִּצְפָּה הוּא

יִבְנֶנּוּ וִיטַלְלֶנּוּ וְיַעֲמִידוּ [וְ] [וְיַעֲמִיד]

דַּלְתֹתָיו מַנְעֻלָיו וּבְרִיחָיו וְאֵת

חוֹמַת בְּרֵכַת הַשֶּׁלַח לְגַן־הַמֶּלֶךְ

וְעַד־הַמַּעֲלוֹת הַיּוֹרְדוֹת מֵעִיר

דָּוִיד : ס אַחֲרָיו הֶחֱזִיק נְחֶמְיָה ¹⁶

בֶן־עַזְבּוּק שַׂר חֲצִי פֶּלֶךְ בֵּית־צוּר

official of half the district of Keilah, carried out repairs for his district. [18] After him their brothers carried out repairs *under* Bavvai the son of Henadad, official of *the other* half of the district of Keilah. [19] Next to him Ezer the son of Jeshua, *[a]*the official of Mizpah, repaired [1]another section in front of the ascent of the armory *[b]*at the Angle. [20] After him Baruch the son of Zabbai zealously repaired another section, from the Angle to the doorway of the house of *[a]*Eliashib the high priest. [21] After him Meremoth the son of Uriah the son of Hakkoz repaired another section, from the doorway of Eliashib's house even as far as the end of [1]his house. [22] After him the priests, *[a]*the men of the [1]valley, carried out repairs. [23] After [1]them Benjamin and Hasshub carried out repairs in front of their house. After [1]them Azariah the son of Maaseiah, son of Ananiah, carried out repairs beside his house. [24] After him Binnui the son of Henadad repaired another section, from the house of Azariah as far as *[a]*the Angle and as far as the corner. [25] Palal the son of Uzai *made repairs* in front of the Angle and the tower projecting from the upper house of the king, which is by *[a]*the court of the guard. After him Pedaiah the son of Parosh *made repairs*. [26] *[a]*The temple servants living in *[b]*Ophel *made repairs* as far as the front of *[c]*the Water Gate toward the east and the projecting tower. [27] After [1]them *[a]*the Tekoites repaired another section in front of the great projecting tower and as far as the wall of Ophel.

Neh. 3:28 Above *[a]*the Horse Gate the priests carried out repairs, each in front of his house. [29] After [1]them Zadok the son

עַד־נֶגֶד קִבְרֵי דָוִיד וְעַד־הַבְּרֵכָה
הָעֲשׂוּיָה וְעַד בֵּית הַגִּבֹּרִים׃ ס 17
אַחֲרָיו הֶחֱזִיקוּ הַלְוִיִּם רְחוּם בֶּן־
בָּנִי עַל־יָדוֹ הֶחֱזִיק חֲשַׁבְיָה שַׂר־
חֲצִי־פֶלֶךְ קְעִילָה לְפִלְכּוֹ׃ ס 18
אַחֲרָיו הֶחֱזִיקוּ אֲחֵיהֶם בַּוַּי בֶּן־
חֵנָדָד שַׂר חֲצִי פֶּלֶךְ קְעִילָה׃ ס 19
וַיְחַזֵּק עַל־יָדוֹ עֵזֶר בֶּן־יֵשׁוּעַ שַׂר
הַמִּצְפָּה מִדָּה שֵׁנִית מִנֶּגֶד עֲלֹת
הַנֶּשֶׁק הַמִּקְצֹעַ׃ ס 20 אַחֲרָיו הֶחֱרָה
הֶחֱזִיק בָּרוּךְ בֶּן־זַבַּי [זַכַּי] מִדָּה
שֵׁנִית מִן־הַמִּקְצוֹעַ עַד־פֶּתַח בֵּית
אֶלְיָשִׁיב הַכֹּהֵן הַגָּדוֹל׃ ס 21 אַחֲרָיו
הֶחֱזִיק מְרֵמוֹת בֶּן־אוּרִיָּה בֶּן־הַקּוֹץ
מִדָּה שֵׁנִית מִפֶּתַח בֵּית אֶלְיָשִׁיב
וְעַד־תַּכְלִית בֵּית אֶלְיָשִׁיב׃ ס 22
וְאַחֲרָיו הֶחֱזִיקוּ הַכֹּהֲנִים אַנְשֵׁי
הַכִּכָּר׃ 23 אַחֲרָיו הֶחֱזִיק בִּנְיָמִן
וְחַשּׁוּב נֶגֶד בֵּיתָם ס אַחֲרָיו הֶחֱזִיק
עֲזַרְיָה בֶן־מַעֲשֵׂיָה בֶּן־עֲנָנְיָה אֵצֶל
בֵּיתוֹ׃ ס 24 אַחֲרָיו הֶחֱזִיק בִּנּוּי בֶּן־
חֵנָדָד מִדָּה שֵׁנִית מִבֵּית עֲזַרְיָה
עַד־הַמִּקְצוֹעַ וְעַד־הַפִּנָּה׃ 25 פָּלָל
בֶּן־אוּזַי מִנֶּגֶד הַמִּקְצוֹעַ וְהַמִּגְדָּל
הַיּוֹצֵא מִבֵּית הַמֶּלֶךְ הָעֶלְיוֹן אֲשֶׁר
לַחֲצַר הַמַּטָּרָה אַחֲרָיו פְּדָיָה בֶן־
פַּרְעֹשׁ׃ ס 26 וְהַנְּתִינִים הָיוּ יֹשְׁבִים
בָּעֹפֶל עַד נֶגֶד שַׁעַר הַמַּיִם לַמִּזְרָח

of Immer carried out repairs in front of his house. And after him Shemaiah the son of Shecaniah, the keeper of the East Gate, carried out repairs. **30** After him Hananiah the son of Shelemiah, and Hanun the sixth son of Zalaph, repaired another section. After him Meshullam the son of Berechiah carried out repairs in front of his own [1]quarters. **31** After him Malchijah, [1]one of [a]the goldsmiths, carried out repairs as far as the house of the temple servants and of the merchants, in front of the [2]Inspection Gate and as far as the upper room of the corner. **32** Between the upper room of the corner and [a]the Sheep Gate the goldsmiths and the merchants carried out repairs.

27 אַחֲרָיו ס : וְהַמִּגְדָּל הַיּוֹצֵא הֶחֱזִיקוּ הַתְּקֹעִים מִדָּה שֵׁנִית מִנֶּגֶד הַמִּגְדָּל הַגָּדוֹל הַיּוֹצֵא וְעַד חוֹמַת הָעֹפֶל : 28 מֵעַל ׀ שַׁעַר הַסּוּסִים הֶחֱזִיקוּ הַכֹּהֲנִים אִישׁ לְנֶגֶד בֵּיתוֹ : 29 אַחֲרָיו הֶחֱזִיק צָדוֹק בֶּן אִמֵּר נֶגֶד בֵּיתוֹ ס וְאַחֲרָיו הֶחֱזִיק שְׁמַעְיָה בֶן שְׁכַנְיָה שֹׁמֵר שַׁעַר הַמִּזְרָח : 30 ס אַחֲרֵי [אַחֲרָיו] הֶחֱזִיק חֲנַנְיָה בֶן שֶׁלֶמְיָה וְחָנוּן בֶּן צָלָף הַשִּׁשִּׁי מִדָּה שֵׁנִי ס אַחֲרָיו הֶחֱזִיק מְשֻׁלָּם בֶּן בֶּרֶכְיָה נֶגֶד נִשְׁכָּתוֹ : 31 ס אַחֲרֵי [אַחֲרָיו] הֶחֱזִיק מַלְכִּיָּה בֶּן הַצֹּרְפִי עַד בֵּית הַנְּתִינִים וְהָרֹכְלִים נֶגֶד שַׁעַר הַמִּפְקָד וְעַד עֲלִיַּת הַפִּנָּה : 32 וּבֵין עֲלִיַּת הַפִּנָּה לְשַׁעַר הַצֹּאן הֶחֱזִיקוּ הַצֹּרְפִים וְהָרֹכְלִים : פ

References

Nehemiah 3:1
[1]Lit *it*
[a]Neh 3:20; 13:28
[b]Neh 3:32; 12:39
[c]Neh 6:1; 7:1
[d]Neh 12:39
[e]Jer 31:38

Nehemiah 3:2
[1]Lit *him*
[a]Neh 7:36

Nehemiah 3:3
[a]Neh 12:39

Nehemiah 3:4
[1]Lit *them*

Nehemiah 3:5
[1]Lit *them*
[2]Lit *bring their neck to*

Nehemiah 3:6
[a]Neh 12:39

Nehemiah 3:7
[1]Or *which was under the jurisdiction of the governor* of the province *beyond the River, also made repairs*
[a]Neh 2:7

Nehemiah 3:8
[a]Neh 3:31, 32
[b]Neh 12:38

Nehemiah 3:9
[a]Neh 3:12, 17

Nehemiah 3:19
[1]Lit *a second measure,* and so in vv 20, 21, 24, 30
[a]Neh 3:15
[b]2 Chr 26:9

Nehemiah 3:20
[a]Neh 3:1

Nehemiah 3:21
[1]Lit *Eliashib's*

Nehemiah 3:22
[1]Lit *circle;* i.e. lower Jordan valley
[a]Neh 12:28

Nehemiah 3:23
[1]Lit *him*

Nehemiah 3:24
[a]Neh 3:19

Nehemiah 3:25
[a]Jer 32:2

Nehemiah 3:26
[a]Neh 7:46
[b]Neh 11:21
[c]Neh 8:1

Nehemiah 3:27
[1]Lit *him*
[a]Neh 3:5

Nehemiah 3:28
[a]2 Kin 11:16; 2 Chr 23:15; Jer 31:40

Nehemiah 3:11 [a]Neh 12:38	**Nehemiah 3:29** [1]Lit *him*
Nehemiah 3:12 [a]Neh 3:9	**Nehemiah 3:30** [1]Or *cell*
Nehemiah 3:13 [1]Lit *Gate of Ash-heaps* [a]Neh 2:13	**Nehemiah 3:31** [1]Lit *son of* [2]Or *Mustering* [a]Neh 3:8, 32
Nehemiah 3:14 [1]Lit *Gate of Ash-heaps* [a]Jer 6:1 [b]Neh 2:13	**Nehemiah 3:32** [a]Neh 3:1; 12:39
Nehemiah 3:15 [a]Neh 2:17 [b]2 Kin 25:4 [c]Neh 12:37	
Nehemiah 3:16 [a]Neh 3:9, 12, 17 [b]2 Kin 20:20; Is 7:3	

Process of Discovery

Linguistics Section

Linguistic Structure

Neh. 3:1 Then [a]Eliashib the high priest arose with his brothers the priests and built [b]the Sheep Gate; they consecrated it and [c]hung its doors. They consecrated [1]the wall to [d]the Tower of the Hundred *and* [e]the Tower of Hananel. **2** Next to him [a]the men of Jericho built, and next to [1]them Zaccur the son of Imri built.

Neh. 3:3 Now the sons of Hassenaah built [a]the Fish Gate; they laid its beams and hung its doors with its bolts and bars. **4** Next to them Meremoth the son of Uriah the son of Hakkoz made repairs. And next to him Meshullam the son of Berechiah the son of Meshezabel made repairs. And next to [1]him Zadok the son of Baana *also* made repairs. **5** Moreover, next to [1]him the Tekoites made repairs, but their nobles did not [2]support the work of their masters.

Neh. 3:6 Joiada the son of Paseah and Meshullam the son of Besodeiah repaired [a]the Old Gate; they laid its beams and hung its doors with its bolts and its bars. **7** Next to them Melatiah the Gibeonite and Jadon the Meronothite, the men of Gibeon and of Mizpah, [1]also made repairs for the official seat of the [a]governor *of the province* beyond the River. **8** Next to him Uzziel the son of Harhaiah of the [a]goldsmiths made repairs. And next to him Hananiah, one of the perfumers, made repairs, and they restored Jerusalem as far as [b]the Broad Wall. **9** Next to them Rephaiah the son of Hur, [a]the official of half the district of Jerusalem, made repairs. **10** Next to them Jedaiah the son of Harumaph made repairs opposite his house. And next to him Hattush the son of Hashabneiah made repairs. **11** Malchijah the son of Harim and Hasshub the son of Pahath-moab repaired another section and [a]the Tower of Furnaces. **12** Next to him Shallum the son of Hallohesh, [a]the official of half the district of Jerusalem, made repairs, he and his daughters.

Neh. 3:13 Hanun and the inhabitants of Zanoah repaired [a]the Valley Gate. They built it and hung its doors with its bolts and its bars, and a thousand cubits of the wall to the [1]Refuse Gate.

Neh. 3:14 Malchijah the son of Rechab, the official of the district of [a]Beth-haccherem repaired the [1b]Refuse Gate. He built it and hung its doors with its bolts and its bars.

Neh. 3:15 Shallum the son of Col-hozeh, the official of the district of Mizpah, [a]repaired the Fountain Gate. He built it, covered it and hung its doors with its bolts and its bars, and the wall of the Pool of Shelah at [b]the king's garden as far as [c]the steps that descend from the city of David. **16** After him Nehemiah the son of Azbuk, *a*official of half the district of Beth-zur, made repairs as far as *a point* opposite the tombs of David, and as far as *b*the artificial pool and the house of the mighty men. **17** After him the Levites carried out repairs *under* Rehum the son of Bani. Next to him Hashabiah, the official of half the district of Keilah, carried out repairs for his district. **18** After him their brothers carried out repairs *under* Bavvai the son of Henadad, official of *the other* half of the district of Keilah. **19** Next to him Ezer the son of Jeshua, *a*the official of Mizpah, repaired *1*another section in front of the ascent of the armory *b*at the Angle. **20** After him Baruch the son of Zabbai zealously repaired another section, from the Angle to the doorway of the house of *a*Eliashib the high priest. **21** After him Meremoth the son of Uriah the son of Hakkoz repaired another section, from the doorway of Eliashib's house even as far as the end of *1*his house. **22** After him the priests, *a*the men of the *1*valley, carried out repairs. **23** After *1*them Benjamin and Hasshub carried out repairs in front of their house. After *1*them Azariah the son of Maaseiah, son of Ananiah, carried out repairs beside his house. **24** After him Binnui the son of Henadad repaired another section, from the house of Azariah as far as *a*the Angle and as far as the corner. **25** Palal the son of Uzai *made repairs* in front of the Angle and the tower projecting from the upper house of the king, which is by *a*the court of the guard. After him Pedaiah the son of Parosh *made repairs.* **26** *a*The temple servants living in *b*Ophel *made repairs* as far as the front of *c*the Water Gate toward the east and the projecting tower. **27** After *1*them *a*the Tekoites repaired another section in front of the great projecting tower and as far as the wall of Ophel.

Neh. 3:28 Above *a*the Horse Gate the priests carried out repairs, each in front of his house. **29** After *1*them Zadok the son of Immer carried out repairs in front of his house. And after him Shemaiah the son of Shecaniah, the keeper of the East Gate, carried out repairs. **30** After him Hananiah the son of Shelemiah, and Hanun the sixth son of Zalaph, repaired another section. After him Meshullam the son of Berechiah carried out repairs in front of his own *1*quarters. **31** After him Malchijah, *1*one of *a*the goldsmiths, carried out repairs as far as the house of the temple servants and of the merchants, in front of the *2*Inspection Gate and as far as the upper room of the corner. **32** Between the upper room of the corner and *a*the Sheep Gate the goldsmiths and the merchants carried out repairs.

Discussion

The Hebrew version of Nehemiah has chapter three continuing for eight additional verses. These verses will be added to chapter four. This chapter gives the work assignments to the different groups of Jews who were rebuilding the walls of Jerusalem. The people identified were the leaders of each rebuilding group. Nehemiah was able to get the artisans to work on the gate and walls. The gate and walls of the city were necessary for defense and to keep animals either inside the city or outside the city. If the walls remained down, then fewer people would have traveled from Babylon to Jerusalem. Once the walls were completed, Nehemiah believed that more Hebrews would leave their Babylonian homes in favor of being in the Promised Land.

Chapter Four

Language

New American Standard 1995	Hebrew
Neh. 4:1 [1]Now it came about that when [a]Sanballat heard that we were rebuilding the wall, he became furious and very angry and mocked the Jews. [2] He spoke in the presence of his brothers and [a]the [1]wealthy *men* of Samaria and said, "What are these feeble Jews doing? Are they going to restore *it* for themselves? Can they offer sacrifices? Can they finish in a day? Can they revive the stones from the [2b]dusty rubble even the burned ones?" [3] Now Tobiah the Ammonite *was* near him and he said, "Even what they are building — [a]if a fox should [1]jump on *it,* he would break their stone wall down!" **Neh. 4:4** [a]Hear, O our God, how we are despised! [b]Return their reproach on their own heads and give them up for plunder in a land of captivity. [5] Do not [1a]forgive their iniquity and let not their sin be blotted out before You, for they have [2]demoralized the builders. **Neh. 4:6** So we built the wall and the whole wall was joined together to half its *height,* for the people had a [1]mind to work. **Neh. 4:7** [1]Now when Sanballat, Tobiah, the Arabs, the Ammonites and the Ashdodites heard that the [2]repair of the walls of Jerusalem went on, *and* that the	33 וַיְהִ֗י כַּאֲשֶׁ֤ר שָׁמַע֙ סַנְבַלַּ֔ט כִּֽי־אֲנַ֥חְנוּ בוֹנִים֙ אֶת־הַ֣חוֹמָ֔ה וַיִּ֣חַר ל֔וֹ וַיִּכְעַ֖ס הַרְבֵּ֑ה וַיַּלְעֵ֖ג עַל־הַיְּהוּדִֽים׃ 34 וַיֹּ֣אמֶר לִפְנֵ֣י אֶחָ֗יו וְחֵיל֙ שֹֽׁמְר֔וֹן וַיֹּ֕אמֶר מָ֛ה הַיְּהוּדִ֥ים הָאֲמֵלָלִ֖ים עֹשִׂ֑ים הֲיַעַזְב֨וּ לָהֶ֤ם הֲיִזְבָּ֙חוּ֙ הַיְכַלּ֣וּ בַיּ֔וֹם הַיְחַיּ֧וּ אֶת־הָאֲבָנִ֛ים מֵעֲרֵמ֥וֹת הֶעָפָ֖ר וְהֵ֥מָּה שְׂרוּפֽוֹת׃ 35 וְטוֹבִיָּ֥ה הָעַמֹּנִ֖י אֶצְל֑וֹ וַיֹּ֗אמֶר גַּ֤ם אֲשֶׁר־הֵם֙ בּוֹנִ֔ים אִם־יַעֲלֶ֣ה שׁוּעָ֔ל וּפָרַ֖ץ חוֹמַ֥ת אַבְנֵיהֶֽם׃ פ 36 שְׁמַ֤ע אֱלֹהֵ֙ינוּ֙ כִּֽי־הָיִ֣ינוּ בוּזָ֔ה וְהָשֵׁ֥ב חֶרְפָּתָ֖ם אֶל־רֹאשָׁ֑ם וּתְנֵ֥ם לְבִזָּ֖ה בְּאֶ֥רֶץ שִׁבְיָֽה׃ 37 וְאַל־תְּכַס֙ עַל־עֲוֺנָ֔ם וְחַטָּאתָ֖ם מִלְּפָנֶ֣יךָ אַל־תִּמָּחֶ֑ה כִּ֥י הִכְעִ֖יסוּ לְנֶ֥גֶד הַבּוֹנִֽים׃ 38 וַנִּבְנֶה֙ אֶת־הַ֣חוֹמָ֔ה וַתִּקָּשֵׁ֥ר כָּל־הַחוֹמָ֖ה עַד־חֶצְיָ֑הּ וַיְהִ֥י לֵ֥ב לָעָ֖ם לַעֲשֽׂוֹת׃ פ **Neh. 4:1** וַיְהִ֞י כַּאֲשֶׁ֣ר שָׁמַ֣ע סַנְבַלַּ֗ט וְטוֹבִיָּ֤ה וְהָעַרְבִים֙ וְהָעַמֹּנִ֔ים וְהָאַשְׁדּוֹדִ֗ים כִּֽי־עָלְתָ֤ה אֲרוּכָה֙ לְחֹמ֣וֹת יְרוּשָׁלִַ֔ם כִּֽי־הֵחֵ֥לּוּ הַפְּרֻצִ֖ים לְהִסָּתֵ֑ם [2]וַיִּ֥חַר לָהֶ֖ם מְאֹֽד׃ וַיִּקְשְׁר֤וּ כֻלָּם֙ יַחְדָּ֔ו לָב֥וֹא לְהִלָּחֵ֖ם בִּירוּשָׁלִָ֑ם וְלַעֲשׂ֥וֹת ל֖וֹ [3]תּוֹעָֽה׃ וַנִּתְפַּלֵּ֣ל אֶל־אֱלֹהֵ֔ינוּ וַנַּעֲמִ֧יד

breaches began to be closed, they were very angry. [8] All of them *a*conspired together to come *and* fight against Jerusalem and to cause a disturbance in it. [9] But we prayed to our God, and because of them we *a*set up a guard against them day and night.

Neh. 4:10 Thus [1]in Judah it was said,

"The strength of the burden bearers is failing,

Yet there is much [2]rubbish;

And we ourselves are unable

To rebuild the wall."

[11] Our enemies said, "They will not know or see until we come among them, kill them and put a stop to the work." [12] When the Jews who lived near them came and told us ten times, "[1]They will come up against us from every place where you may turn," [13] then I stationed *men* in the lowest parts of the space behind the wall, the [1]exposed places, and I *a*stationed the people in families with their swords, spears and bows. [14] When I saw *their fear,* I rose and spoke to the nobles, the officials and the rest of the people: "*a*Do not be afraid of them; remember the Lord who is great and awesome, and *b*fight for your brothers, your sons, your daughters, your wives and your houses."

Neh. 4:15 When our enemies heard that it was known to us, and that *a*God had frustrated their plan, then all of us returned to the wall, each one to his work. [16] From that day on, half of my servants carried on the work while half of them held the spears, the shields, the bows and the breastplates; and the captains *were* behind the whole house of Judah. [17]

מִשְׁמָר עֲלֵיהֶם יוֹמָם וָלַיְלָה מִפְּנֵיהֶם:

4 וַיֹּאמֶר יְהוּדָה כָּשַׁל כֹּחַ הַסַּבָּל

וְהֶעָפָר הַרְבֵּה וַאֲנַחְנוּ לֹא נוּכַל לִבְנוֹת

5 בַּחוֹמָה: וַיֹּאמְרוּ צָרֵינוּ לֹא יֵדְעוּ

וְלֹא יִרְאוּ עַד אֲשֶׁר נָבוֹא אֶל תּוֹכָם

6 וַהֲרַגְנוּם וְהִשְׁבַּתְנוּ אֶת הַמְּלָאכָה:

וַיְהִי כַּאֲשֶׁר בָּאוּ הַיְּהוּדִים הַיֹּשְׁבִים

אֶצְלָם וַיֹּאמְרוּ לָנוּ עֶשֶׂר פְּעָמִים מִכָּל

7 הַמְּקֹמוֹת אֲשֶׁר תָּשׁוּבוּ עָלֵינוּ:

וָאַעֲמִיד מִתַּחְתִּיּוֹת לַמָּקוֹם מֵאַחֲרֵי

לַחוֹמָה בַּצְּחִיחִים [בַּ][צְּחִיחִים]

וָאַעֲמִיד אֶת הָעָם לְמִשְׁפָּחוֹת עִם

8 חַרְבֹתֵיהֶם רָמְחֵיהֶם וְקַשְּׁתֹתֵיהֶם:

וָאֵרֶא וָאָקוּם וָאֹמַר אֶל הַחֹרִים וְאֶל

הַסְּגָנִים וְאֶל יֶתֶר הָעָם אַל תִּירְאוּ

מִפְּנֵיהֶם אֶת אֲדֹנָי הַגָּדוֹל וְהַנּוֹרָא זְכֹרוּ

וְהִלָּחֲמוּ עַל אֲחֵיכֶם בְּנֵיכֶם וּבְנֹתֵיכֶם

9 נְשֵׁיכֶם וּבָתֵּיכֶם: פ וַיְהִי כַּאֲשֶׁר

שָׁמְעוּ אוֹיְבֵינוּ כִּי נוֹדַע לָנוּ וַיָּפֶר

הָאֱלֹהִים אֶת עֲצָתָם וַנָּשׁוב [וַ][נָּשָׁב]

כֻּלָּנוּ אֶל הַחוֹמָה אִישׁ אֶל מְלַאכְתּוֹ:

10 וַיְהִי מִן הַיּוֹם הַהוּא חֲצִי נְעָרַי

עֹשִׂים בַּמְּלָאכָה וְחֶצְיָם מַחֲזִיקִים

וְהָרְמָחִים הַמָּגִנִּים וְהַקְּשָׁתוֹת וְהַשִּׁרְיֹנִים

11 וְהַשָּׂרִים אַחֲרֵי כָּל בֵּית יְהוּדָה:

הַבּוֹנִים בַּחוֹמָה וְהַנֹּשְׂאִים בַּסֶּבֶל

עֹמְשִׂים בְּאַחַת יָדוֹ עֹשֶׂה בַמְּלָאכָה

12 וְהַבּוֹנִים: וְאַחַת מַחֲזֶקֶת הַשָּׁלַח:

אִישׁ חַרְבּוֹ אֲסוּרִים עַל מָתְנָיו וּבוֹנִים

13 וָאֹמַר אֶל וְהַתּוֹקֵעַ בַּשּׁוֹפָר אֶצְלִי:

הַחֹרִים וְאֶל הַסְּגָנִים וְאֶל יֶתֶר הָעָם

Those who were rebuilding the wall and those who carried burdens took *their* load with one hand doing the work and the other holding a weapon. [18] As for the builders, each *wore* his sword girded at his side as he built, while [1]the trumpeter *stood* near me. [19] I said to the nobles, the officials and the rest of the people, "The work is great and extensive, and we are separated on the wall far from one another. [20] "At whatever place you hear the sound of the trumpet, [1]rally to us there. [a]Our God will fight for us."

Neh. 4:21 So we carried on the work with half of them holding spears from [1]dawn until the stars [2]appeared. [22] At that time I also said to the people, "Let each man with his servant spend the night within Jerusalem so that they may be a guard for us by night and a laborer by day." [23] So neither I, my brothers, my servants, nor the men of the guard who followed me, none of us removed our clothes, each *took* his weapon *even to* the water.

הַמְּלָאכָה הַרְבֵּה וּרְחָבָה וַאֲנַחְנוּ
נִפְרָדִים עַל־הַחוֹמָה רְחוֹקִים אִישׁ
מֵאָחִיו: [14] בַּמָּקוֹם אֲשֶׁר תִּשְׁמְעוּ אֶת־
קוֹל הַשּׁוֹפָר שָׁמָּה תִּקָּבְצוּ אֵלֵינוּ
אֱלֹהֵינוּ יִלָּחֶם לָנוּ: [15] וַאֲנַחְנוּ עֹשִׂים
בַּמְּלָאכָה וְחֶצְיָם מַחֲזִיקִים בָּרְמָחִים
[16] מֵעֲלוֹת הַשַּׁחַר עַד צֵאת הַכּוֹכָבִים:
גַּם בָּעֵת הַהִיא אָמַרְתִּי לָעָם אִישׁ וְנַעֲרוֹ
יָלִינוּ בְּתוֹךְ יְרוּשָׁלִָם וְהָיוּ־לָנוּ הַלַּיְלָה
מִשְׁמָר וְהַיּוֹם מְלָאכָה: [17] וְאֵין אֲנִי
וְאַחַי וּנְעָרַי וְאַנְשֵׁי הַמִּשְׁמָר אֲשֶׁר אַחֲרַי
אֵין־אֲנַחְנוּ פֹשְׁטִים בְּגָדֵינוּ אִישׁ שִׁלְחוֹ
הַמָּיִם: ס

References

<table>
<tr><td valign="top">

Nehemiah 4:1
[1]Ch 3:33 in Heb
[a]Neh 2:10

Nehemiah 4:2
[1]Or *army*
[2]Lit *heaps of dust*
[a]Ezra 4:9, 10
[b]Neh 4:10

Nehemiah 4:3
[1]Lit *go up*
[a]Lam 5:18

Nehemiah 4:4
[a]Ps 123:3, 4
[b]Ps 79:12

Nehemiah 4:5
[1]Lit *cover*
[2]Lit *offended against*
[a]Ps 69:27, 28; Jer 18:23

Nehemiah 4:6
[1]Lit *heart*

Nehemiah 4:7
[1]Ch 4:1 in Heb
[2]Lit *healing*

Nehemiah 4:8
[a]Ps 83:3

</td><td valign="top">

Nehemiah 4:9
[a]Neh 4:11

Nehemiah 4:10
[1]Lit *Judah said*
[2]Lit *dust*

Nehemiah 4:12
[1]So Gr; Heb omits *they...up*

Nehemiah 4:13
[1]Lit *bare*
[a]Neh 4:17, 18

Nehemiah 4:14
[a]Num 14:9; Deut 1:29, 30
[b]2 Sam 10:12

Nehemiah 4:15
[a]2 Sam 17:14

Nehemiah 4:18
[1]Lit *he who sounded the trumpet*

Nehemiah 4:20
[1]Lit *assemble yourselves*
[a]Ex 14:14; Deut 1:30

Nehemiah 4:21
[1]Lit *rising of the dawn*
[2]Lit *came out*

</td></tr>
</table>

Process of Discovery

Linguistics Section

Linguistic Structure

A [1]   [1]Now it came about that when [a]Sanballat heard that we were rebuilding the wall, he became furious and very angry and mocked the Jews. **2** He spoke in the presence of his brothers and [a]the [1]wealthy *men* of Samaria and said, "What are these feeble Jews doing? Are they going to restore *it* for themselves? Can they offer sacrifices? Can they finish in a day? Can they revive the stones from the [2b]dusty rubble even the burned ones?" **3** Now Tobiah the Ammonite *was* near him and he said, "Even what they are building — [a]if a fox should [1]jump on *it,* he would break their stone wall down!"

> **B** [4]   [a]Hear, O our God, how we are despised! [b]Return their reproach on their own heads and give them up for plunder in a land of captivity. **5** Do not [1a]forgive their iniquity and let not their sin be blotted out before You, for they have [2]demoralized the builders. **6** So we built the wall and the whole wall was joined together to half its *height,* for the people had a [1]mind to work.

A' [7] [1]Now when Sanballat, Tobiah, the Arabs, the Ammonites and the Ashdodites heard that the [2]repair of the walls of Jerusalem went on, *and* that the breaches began to be closed, they were very angry. **8** All of them [a]conspired together to come *and* fight against Jerusalem and to cause a disturbance in it. **9** But we prayed to our God, and because of them we [a]set up a guard against them day and night. [10]   Thus [1]in Judah it was said, "The strength of the burden bearers is failing, Yet there is much [2]rubbish; And we ourselves are unable To rebuild the wall." [11] Our enemies said, "They will not know or see until we come among them, kill them and put a stop to the work." **12** When the Jews who lived near them came and told us ten times, "[1]They will come up against us from every place where you may turn,"

> **B'** [13] then I stationed *men* in the lowest parts of the space behind the wall, the [1]exposed places, and I [a]stationed the people in families with their swords, spears and bows. **14** When I saw *their fear,* I rose and spoke to the nobles, the officials and the rest of the people: "[a]Do not be afraid of them; remember the Lord who is great and awesome, and [b]fight for your brothers, your sons, your daughters, your wives and your houses." [15] When our enemies heard that it was known to us, and that [a]God had frustrated their plan, then all of us returned to the wall, each one to his work. **16** From that day on, half of my servants carried on the work while half of them held the spears, the shields, the bows and the breastplates; and the captains *were* behind the whole house of Judah. **17** Those who were rebuilding the wall and those who carried burdens took *their* load with

one hand doing the work and the other holding a weapon. [18] As for the builders, each *wore* his sword girded at his side as he built, while [1]the trumpeter *stood* near me. [19] I said to the nobles, the officials and the rest of the people, "The work is great and extensive, and we are separated on the wall far from one another. [20] "At whatever place you hear the sound of the trumpet, [1]rally to us there. [a]Our God will fight for us." [21] So we carried on the work with half of them holding spears from [1]dawn until the stars [2]appeared. [22] At that time I also said to the people, "Let each man with his servant spend the night within Jerusalem so that they may be a guard for us by night and a laborer by day." [23] So neither I, my brothers, my servants, nor the men of the guard who followed me, none of us removed our clothes, each *took* his weapon *even to* the water.

Discussion

This chapter forms an A-B-A'-B' chiasm. This chapter describes the resistance that came to Jerusalem to prevent the rebuilding of the walls and the Temple.

Questioning the Passage

1. Who were the Jews who lived near Jerusalem? (v. 6)

   Nehemiah said that there were Jews who gathered with his enemies to stop rebuilding the city walls. These Jews broke down and decided not to betray their brethren by attacking them. Instead, these Jews warned Nehemiah about what was about to happen.

2. Why did Nehemiah mention the aristocrats taking up arms? (v. 8)

   Usually, the aristocrats of a city did not join the army to fight an enemy. In this case, the aristocrats of Jerusalem came together with the army to fight.

Biblical Personalities

1. Ammonites – "Ammonite, any member of an ancient Semitic people whose principal city was Rabbath Ammon, in Palestine. The "sons of Ammon" were

in perennial, though sporadic, conflict with the Israelites. After a long period of seminomadic existence, the Ammonites established a kingdom north of Moab in the 13th century BC. With difficulty, their fortress capital was captured by Israel's King David. An Ammonite woman, one of many foreigners taken into Israel's King Solomon's harem, was responsible for inducing the king to worship the Ammonite god Malcom."[15]

2. Ashdodites – "Ashdod (Hebrew: ◀אַשְׁדּוֹד; Arabic: أشدود) is the sixth-largest city and the largest port in Israel accounting for 60% of the country's imported goods. Ashdod is located in the Southern District of the country, on the Mediterranean coast where it is situated between Tel Aviv to the north 32 kilometres (20 miles) away, and Ashkelon to the south 20 km (12 mi) away. Jerusalem is 53 km (33 mi) to the east. The city is also an important regional industrial center."[16]

Culture Section

Questioning the passage

1. What does "if a fox should jump on it, he would break their stone wall down" means? (v. 3)

   The walls of Jerusalem were originally very thick and difficult to breech. The people who lived in Jerusalem at the time of the rebuilding of the walls were mainly poor peasants. They gave what they could to the rebuilding project. Therefore, their new wall was not thick and was weak. This phrase was an insult to the work of rebuilding the wall. It was

---

[15] "Ammonite," Encyclopædia Britannica (Encyclopædia Britannica, inc.), accessed April 24, 2021, https://www.britannica.com/topic/Ammonite.

[16] "Ashdod," Wikipedia (Wikimedia Foundation, April 5, 2021), https://en.wikipedia.org/wiki/Ashdod.

somewhat porous that the weight of a fox would cause the wall to tumble. Walls were placed around cities to protect them from invaders. The walls built by the peasants would not stop anyone, not even a small animal like a fox.[17]

2. What is Nehemiah asking for in verse five?

Nehemiah was so angry at Sanballat and Tobiah that he prayed to the LORD not to forgive their actions. They had hindered the rebuilding of the walls of Jerusalem. So, Nehemiah invoked the LORD's name to blot out their existence from history. Nehemiah placed a curse on Sanballat and Tobiah.[18]

Thoughts

This chapter describes the situation in Jerusalem during the rebuilding of the walls. Men had to carry spears and swords while working on the wall. They did not know when their enemies might attack. Also, a night watch had to be kept. It was not common to attack a city at night. However, Nehemiah feared that this might happen. Therefore, he posted guards.

---

[17] Rocco A. Errico and George M. Lamsa, *Aramaic Light on Ezra Through the Song of Solomon* (Smyrna, GA: Noohra Foundation, 2010).
[18] IBID.

Chapter Five

Language

New American Standard 1995	Hebrew

Neh. 5:1 Now [a]there was a great outcry of the people and of their wives against their [b]Jewish brothers. **2** For there were those who said, "We, our sons and our daughters are many; therefore let us [a]get grain that we may eat and live." **3** There were others who said, "We are mortgaging our fields, our vineyards and our houses that we might get grain because of the famine." **4** Also there were those who said, "We have borrowed money [a]for the King's tax *on* our fields and our vineyards. **5** "Now [a]our flesh is like the flesh of our brothers, our children like their children. Yet behold, [b]we are forcing our sons and our daughters to be slaves, and some of our daughters are forced into bondage *already,* and [1]we are helpless because our fields and vineyards belong to others."

Neh. 5:6 Then I was very [a]angry when I had heard their outcry and these words. **7** I consulted with myself and contended with the nobles and the rulers and said to them, "[a]You are exacting usury, each from his brother!" Therefore, I held a great assembly against them. **8** I said to them, "We according to our ability [a]have [1]redeemed our Jewish brothers who were sold to the nations; now would you even sell your brothers that they may be sold to us?" Then they were silent and could

וַתְּהִ֨י צַעֲקַ֥ת הָעָ֛ם וּנְשֵׁיהֶ֖ם Neh. 5:1
גְּדוֹלָ֑ה אֶל־אֲחֵיהֶ֖ם הַיְּהוּדִֽים׃ 2
וְיֵ֤שׁ אֲשֶׁר֙ אֹמְרִ֔ים בָּנֵ֥ינוּ וּבְנֹתֵ֖ינוּ
אֲנַ֣חְנוּ רַבִּ֑ים וְנִקְחָ֥ה דָגָ֖ן וְנֹאכְלָ֥ה
וְנִחְיֶֽה׃ 3 וְיֵשׁ֙ אֲשֶׁ֣ר אֹמְרִ֔ים שְׂדֹתֵ֛ינוּ
וּכְרָמֵ֥ינוּ וּבָתֵּ֖ינוּ אֲנַ֣חְנוּ עֹרְבִ֑ים
וְנִקְחָ֥ה דָגָ֖ן בָּרָעָֽב׃ 4 וְיֵשׁ֙ אֲשֶׁ֣ר
אֹמְרִ֔ים לָוִ֥ינוּ כֶ֖סֶף לְמִדַּ֣ת הַמֶּ֑לֶךְ
שְׂדֹתֵ֖ינוּ וּכְרָמֵֽינוּ׃ 5 וְעַתָּ֗ה כִּבְשַׂ֤ר
אַחֵ֙ינוּ֙ בְּשָׂרֵ֔נוּ כִּבְנֵיהֶ֖ם בָּנֵ֑ינוּ וְהִנֵּ֣ה
אֲנַ֣חְנוּ כֹבְשִׁ֗ים אֶת־בָּנֵ֤ינוּ וְאֶת־
בְּנֹתֵ֙ינוּ֙ לַעֲבָדִ֔ים וְיֵ֥שׁ מִבְּנֹתֵ֖ינוּ
נִכְבָּשׁ֔וֹת וְאֵ֣ין לְאֵ֣ל יָדֵ֔נוּ וּשְׂדֹתֵ֥ינוּ
וּכְרָמֵ֖ינוּ לַאֲחֵרִֽים׃ 6 וַיִּ֥חַר לִ֖י מְאֹ֑ד
כַּאֲשֶׁ֤ר שָׁמַ֙עְתִּי֙ אֶת־זַעֲקָתָ֔ם וְאֵ֖ת
הַדְּבָרִ֥ים הָאֵֽלֶּה׃ 7 וַיִּמָּלֵ֨ךְ לִבִּ֜י עָלַ֗י
וָאָרִ֙יבָה֙ אֶת־הַחֹרִ֣ים וְאֶת־הַסְּגָנִ֔ים
וָאֹמְרָ֣ה לָהֶ֔ם מַשָּׁ֥א אִישׁ־בְּאָחִ֖יו
אַתֶּ֣ם נֹשִׁ֑אים [נֹשִׁ֖ים] וָאֶתֵּ֥ן עֲלֵיהֶ֖ם
קְהִלָּ֥ה גְדוֹלָֽה׃ 8 וָאֹמְרָ֣ה לָהֶ֗ם
אֲנַ֣חְנוּ קָנִ֗ינוּ אֶת־אַחֵ֨ינוּ הַיְּהוּדִ֜ים
הַנִּמְכָּרִ֤ים לַגּוֹיִם֙ כְּדֵ֣י בָ֔נוּ וְגַם־אַתֶּ֛ם
תִּמְכְּר֥וּ אֶת־אֲחֵיכֶ֖ם וְנִמְכְּרוּ־לָ֑נוּ

not find a word *to say*. [9] Again I said, "The thing which you are doing is not good; should you not walk in the fear of our God because of [a]the reproach of the nations, our enemies? [10] "And likewise I, my brothers and my servants are lending them money and grain. Please, let us leave off this usury. [11] "Please, give back to them this very day their fields, their vineyards, their olive groves and their houses, also the hundredth *part* of the money and of the grain, the new wine and the oil that you are exacting from them." [12] Then they said, "We [a]will give *it* back and [b]will require nothing from them; we will do exactly as you say." So I called the priests and [c]took an oath from them that they would do according to this [1]promise. [13] I [a]also shook out the [1]front of my garment and said, "Thus may God shake out every man from his house and from his possessions who does not fulfill this [2]promise; even thus may he be shaken out and emptied." And [b]all the assembly said, "Amen!" And they praised the LORD. Then the people did according to this [2]promise.

Neh. 5:14 Moreover, from the day that I was appointed to be their governor in the land of Judah, from [a]the twentieth year to the [b]thirty-second year of King Artaxerxes, *for* twelve years, neither I nor my [1]kinsmen have eaten the governor's food *allowance*. [15] But the former governors who were before me [1]laid burdens on the people and took from them bread and wine besides forty shekels of silver; even their servants domineered the people. But I did not do so [a]because of the fear of God. [16] I also

וַיַּחֲרִישׁוּ וְלֹא מָצְאוּ דָּבָר ‪:‬ ס ‪9‬

וָאוֹמַר [וָ][אוֹמַר] לֹא־טוֹב הַדָּבָר

אֲשֶׁר־אַתֶּם עֹשִׂים הֲלוֹא בְּיִרְאַת

אֱלֹהֵינוּ תֵּלֵכוּ מֵחֶרְפַּת הַגּוֹיִם

אוֹיְבֵינוּ ‪:‬ ‪10‬ וְגַם־אֲנִי אַחַי וּנְעָרַי

נֹשִׁים בָּהֶם כֶּסֶף וְדָגָן נַעַזְבָה־נָּא

אֶת־הַמַּשָּׁא הַזֶּה ‪:‬ ‪11‬ הָשִׁיבוּ נָא לָהֶם

כְּהַיּוֹם שְׂדֹתֵיהֶם כַּרְמֵיהֶם זֵיתֵיהֶם

וּבָתֵּיהֶם וּמְאַת הַכֶּסֶף וְהַדָּגָן

הַתִּירוֹשׁ וְהַיִּצְהָר אֲשֶׁר אַתֶּם נֹשִׁים

בָּהֶם ‪:‬ ‪12‬ וַיֹּאמְרוּ נָשִׁיב וּמֵהֶם לֹא

נְבַקֵּשׁ כֵּן נַעֲשֶׂה כַּאֲשֶׁר אַתָּה אוֹמֵר

וָאֶקְרָא אֶת־הַכֹּהֲנִים וָאַשְׁבִּיעֵם

לַעֲשׂוֹת כַּדָּבָר הַזֶּה ‪:‬ ‪13‬ גַּם־חָצְנִי

נָעַרְתִּי וָאֹמְרָה כָּכָה יְנַעֵר

הָאֱלֹהִים אֶת־כָּל־הָאִישׁ אֲשֶׁר לֹא־

יָקִים אֶת־הַדָּבָר הַזֶּה מִבֵּיתוֹ

וּמִיגִיעוֹ וְכָכָה יִהְיֶה נָעוּר וָרֵק

וַיֹּאמְרוּ כָל־הַקָּהָל אָמֵן וַיְהַלְלוּ

אֶת־יְהוָה וַיַּעַשׂ הָעָם כַּדָּבָר הַזֶּה ‪:‬

‪14‬ גַּם מִיּוֹם ׀ אֲשֶׁר־צִוָּה אֹתִי לִהְיוֹת

פֶּחָם בְּאֶרֶץ יְהוּדָה מִשְּׁנַת עֶשְׂרִים

וְעַד שְׁנַת שְׁלֹשִׁים וּשְׁתַּיִם

לְאַרְתַּחְשַׁסְתְּא הַמֶּלֶךְ שָׁנִים שְׁתֵּים

עֶשְׂרֵה אֲנִי וְאַחַי לֶחֶם הַפֶּחָה לֹא

אָכַלְתִּי ‪:‬ ‪15‬ וְהַפַּחוֹת הָרִאשֹׁנִים

אֲשֶׁר־לְפָנַי הִכְבִּידוּ עַל־הָעָם

וַיִּקְחוּ מֵהֶם בְּלֶחֶם וָיַיִן אַחַר כֶּסֶף־

[1]applied myself to the work on this wall; we did not buy any land, and all my servants were gathered there for the work. **17** Moreover, [a]*there were* at my table one hundred and fifty Jews and officials, besides those who came to us from the nations that were around us. **18** Now [a]*that* which was prepared for each day was one ox *and* six choice sheep, also birds were prepared for me; and once in ten days all sorts of wine *were furnished* in abundance. Yet for all this [b]I did not demand the governor's food *allowance,* because the servitude was heavy on this people. **19** [a]Remember me, O my God, for good, *according to* all that I have done for this people.

שְׁקָלִים אַרְבָּעִים גַּם נַעֲרֵיהֶם שָׁלְטוּ עַל־הָעָם וַאֲנִי לֹא־עָשִׂיתִי כֵן מִפְּנֵי יִרְאַת אֱלֹהִים: ‏16 וְגַם בִּמְלֶאכֶת הַחוֹמָה הַזֹּאת הֶחֱזַקְתִּי וְשָׂדֶה לֹא קָנִינוּ וְכָל־נְעָרַי קְבוּצִים שָׁם עַל־הַמְּלָאכָה: ‏17 וְהַיְּהוּדִים וְהַסְּגָנִים מֵאָה וַחֲמִשִּׁים אִישׁ וְהַבָּאִים אֵלֵינוּ מִן־הַגּוֹיִם אֲשֶׁר־סְבִיבֹתֵינוּ עַל־שֻׁלְחָנִי: ‏18 וַאֲשֶׁר הָיָה נַעֲשֶׂה לְיוֹם אֶחָד שׁוֹר אֶחָד צֹאן שֵׁשׁ־בְּרֻרוֹת וְצִפֳּרִים נַעֲשׂוּ־לִי וּבֵין עֲשֶׂרֶת יָמִים בְּכָל־יַיִן לְהַרְבֵּה וְעִם־זֶה לֶחֶם הַפֶּחָה לֹא בִקַּשְׁתִּי כִּי־כָבְדָה הָעֲבֹדָה עַל־הָעָם הַזֶּה: ‏19 זָכְרָה־לִּי אֱלֹהַי לְטוֹבָה כֹּל אֲשֶׁר־עָשִׂיתִי עַל־הָעָם הַזֶּה: פ

References

Nehemiah 5:1 [a]Lev 25:35 [b]Deut 15:7	**Nehemiah 5:13** [1]Lit *bosom* [2]Lit *word* [a]Acts 18:6 [b]Neh 8:6
Nehemiah 5:2 [a]Hag 1:6	**Nehemiah 5:14** [1]Lit *brothers* [a]Neh 1:1 [b]Neh 13:6
Nehemiah 5:4 [a]Ezra 4:13; 7:24	
Nehemiah 5:5 [1]Lit *there is not the power in our hands* [a]Gen 37:27 [b]Lev 25:39	**Nehemiah 5:15** [1]Lit *made heavy* [a]Neh 5:9; Job 31:23
Nehemiah 5:6 [a]Ex 11:8	**Nehemiah 5:16** [1]Or *held fast*
Nehemiah 5:7 [a]Ex 22:25; Lev 25:36; Deut 23:19, 20	**Nehemiah 5:17** [a]1 Kin 18:19
Nehemiah 5:8 [1]Lit *bought* [a]Lev 25:48	**Nehemiah 5:18** [a]1 Kin 4:22, 23 [b]2 Thess 3:8
Nehemiah 5:9 [a]Neh 4:4	
Nehemiah 5:12 [1]Lit *word* [a]2 Chr 28:15 [b]Neh 10:31 [c]Ezra 10:5	

Process of Discovery

Linguistics Section

Linguistic Structure

A [1] Now ᵃthere was a great outcry of the people and of their wives against their ᵇJewish brothers. [2] For there were those who said, "We, our sons and our daughters are many; therefore let us ᵃget grain that we may eat and live." [3] There were others who said, "We are mortgaging our fields, our vineyards and our houses that we might get grain because of the famine." [4] Also there were those who said, "We have borrowed money ᵃfor the King's tax *on* our fields and our vineyards. [5] "Now ᵃour flesh is like the flesh of our brothers, our children like their children. Yet behold, ᵇwe are forcing our sons and our daughters to be slaves, and some of our daughters are forced into bondage *already,* and ¹we are helpless because our fields and vineyards belong to others."

B [6] Then I was very ᵃangry when I had heard their outcry and these words. [7] I consulted with myself and contended with the nobles and the rulers and said to them, "ᵃYou are exacting usury, each from his brother!" Therefore, I held a great assembly against them. [8] I said to them, "We according to our ability ᵃhave ¹redeemed our Jewish brothers who were sold to the nations; now would you even sell your brothers that they may be sold to us?" Then they were silent and could not find a word *to say.*

C [9] Again I said, "The thing which you are doing is not good; should you not walk in the fear of our God because of ᵃthe reproach of the nations, our enemies? [10] "And likewise I, my brothers and my servants are lending them money and grain. Please, let us leave off this usury. [11] "Please, give back to them this very day their fields, their vineyards, their olive groves and their houses, also the hundredth *part* of the money and of the grain, the new wine and the oil that you are exacting from them." [12] Then they said, "We ᵃwill give *it* back and ᵇwill require nothing from them; we will do exactly as you say."

B' So I called the priests and ᶜtook an oath from them that they would do according to this ¹promise. [13] I ᵃalso shook out the ¹front of my garment and said, "Thus may God shake out every man from his house and from his possessions who does not fulfill this [2]promise; even thus may he be shaken out and emptied." And [b]all the assembly said, "Amen!" And they praised the LORD. Then the people did according to this [2]promise.

A' [14] Moreover, from the day that I was appointed to be their governor in the land of Judah, from [a]the twentieth year to the [b]thirty-second year of King Artaxerxes, *for* twelve years, neither I nor my [1]kinsmen have eaten the governor's food *allowance.* [15] But the former governors who were before me [1]laid burdens on the people and took from them bread and wine besides forty shekels of silver; even their servants domineered the people. But I did not do so [a]because of the fear of God. [16] I also [1]applied myself to the work on this wall; we did not buy any land, and all my servants were gathered there for the work. [17] Moreover, [a]*there were* at my table one hundred and fifty Jews and officials, besides those who came to us from the nations that were around us. [18] Now [a]that which was prepared for each day was one ox *and* six choice sheep, also birds were prepared for me; and once in ten days all sorts of wine *were furnished* in abundance. Yet for all this [b]I did not demand the governor's food *allowance,* because the servitude was heavy on this people. [19] [a]Remember me, O my God, for good, *according to* all that I have done for this people.

Discussion

This chapter is an A-B-C chiasm. The center of the chiasm is Nehemiah's commands to the people. The people required resources and used an ancient method of slavery. Nehemiah condemned the people for what they were doing before issuing his commands. The main topic of the chapter is the economic inequity and iniquity of the people in Jerusalem.

Questioning the Passage

1. Why was there an outcry from the people? (v. 1)

   The outcry from the people was because of the economic conditions. Many people had to sell their land to buy the necessities of life. Even worse than that, many had to sell their children into slavery to buy bread.

2. What is verse two referring to?

   The Sage Malbim[ii] said that there were three groups of poor people who were speaking. The first group's complaint was made by the people who did not have land to sell. These people had to sell their children into slavery to go to the market and buy bread. [19]

3. Who was the second group that Malbim identified? (v. 3)

   The second group of complainers was landowners who had to mortgage their farms because they did not have enough money to purchase the bare essentials of life. Their farms were not producing enough grain to feed their own families.

4. Who was the third group that Malbim identified? (v. 4)

   The third group of complainers had already mortgaged their land to pay the Persian taxes.[20]

5. What is the meaning of verse five?

   The Torah permits a Hebrew in desperate circumstances to sell himself or his daughters to a fellow Hebrew as servants. This law can be found in Exodus in the twenty-first chapter. The Exodus regulation is repeated in Leviticus.[21]

   Lev. 25:39 "If a ¹countryman of yours becomes so poor with regard to you that he sells himself to you, you shall not subject him to a slave's service. ⁴⁰ 'He shall be with you as a hired man, as ᵃif he were a sojourner;

---

[19] Nosson Scherman and Meir Zlotowitz, *The Writings = Kesuvim / The Writings: with a Commentary Anthologized from Rabbinic Writings = Ketuvim: 'im Perush Rashi, Metsudat Dayid, Metsudat Tsiyon, ye-'od* (Brooklyn, NY: Mesorah Publications, 2016).

[20] IBID.

[21] IBID.

he shall serve with you until the year of jubilee. [41] 'He shall then go out from you, he and his sons with him, and shall go back to his family, that he may return to the property of his forefathers.

The Torah prohibits a lender from unduly pressuring a borrower for repayment of a loan. This commandment is in Exodus chapter twenty-two.

The Sage Rashi[iiii] said that the phrase "like the flesh of our brethren is our flesh" means that the poor people are as esteemed and distinguished as the rich people. That also includes the children of both rich and poor.[22]

6. What does verse eight mean?

The wealthy Jews purchased many Jews who were sold into slavery to Gentiles in Jerusalem and Judea. Nehemiah asked these wealthy Jews if they intended to sell their purchased Jewish brethren back to the Gentiles. Nehemiah embarrassed these wealthy Jews that they would even consider doing this.[23]

In some English translations, the word "ransom" is used instead of "redeemed." To purchase a Jew from a Gentile was considered redeeming the Jew. The word "ransom" in old English means "shield." Therefore, to pay a ransom for a brother Jew was to protect him from the ways of the Gentiles, thus redeeming him.

---

[22] A. J. Rosenberg, *Daniel, Ezra, Nehemiah: a New English Translation = Sifrê Dānîyyēl, 'Ezrâ, Něhemyā* (New York: Judaica Pr., 1991).
[23] Nosson Scherman and Meir Zlotowitz, *The Writings = Kesuvim / The Writings: with a Commentary Anthologized from Rabbinic Writings = Ketuvim: 'im Perush Rashi, Metsudat Dayid, Metsudat Tsiyon, ye-'od* (Brooklyn, NY: Mesorah Publications, 2016).

7. When was the twentieth and thirty-second year of Artaxerxes' reign? (v. 14)

    Artaxerxes reigned from 464 to 425 BCE. The twentieth year of his reign was 444 BCE. The thirty-second year was 432 BCE.

8. What do forty shekels represent? (v. 15)

    Forty shekels was the yearly tax imposed by the Persian kings on their subjects.

9. What do every ten days a multitude of all sorts of wine mean? (v. 18)

    The Sage Rashi believed that the people drank ten days' worth of wine every day.[24]

Biblical Personalities

1. "Artaxerxes was King of Persia from c. 464 to c. 425 BC. He was a son of King Xerxes (Ahasuerus) and is often referred to as Artaxerxes I Longimanus. Ezra and Nehemiah both traveled from Persia to Jerusalem from the court of Artaxerxes. Although he saw several insurrections over the course of his reign, Artaxerxes' rule is generally regarded as a peaceful one. Due to his tolerant policy toward the Jews in his realm, Artaxerxes played a key role in the rebuilding of the Temple and the wall of Jerusalem."[25]

---

[24] Nosson Scherman and Meir Zlotowitz, *The Writings = Kesuvim / The Writings: with a Commentary Anthologized from Rabbinic Writings = Ketuvim: 'im Perush Rashi, Metsudat Dayid, Metsudat Tsiyon, ye-'od* (Brooklyn, NY: Mesorah Publications, 2016).

[25] GotQuestions.org, "Home," GotQuestions.org, November 29, 2017, https://www.gotquestions.org/Artaxerxes-in-the-Bible.html.

Phrase Study

1. צְעָקָה (seʿāqâ) cry, outcry.

"BDB suggests the original meaning in Arabic was "sound as thunder." This root means to call out for help under great distress or to utter an exclamation in great excitement (cf. 2 Kgs 2:12). E.g., immediately on realizing that the pottage they were contentedly eating was poisonous, the sons of the prophets cried out in anguish (4:40). A woman who is raped is exonerated as long as she cries for help. If she does not, she is guilty of consenting to adultery (Deut 22:23–27). Israel's leaders often had to petition God earnestly for help. As a leader, Moses faced numerous difficult situations which caused him to cry out in desperation to Yahweh for direction (cf. Ex 17:4). One time God's response to Moses was simply for Moses to cease crying and get into action (14:15). Further it describes the response of Esau to the loss of his blessing and of the nation Israel to the loss of the ark of the Philistines (Gen 27:34; 1 Sam 4:14). This word often refers to the cry of those plundered and ravaged in war (cf. Jer 49:21).

A strong outcry frequently indicates that righteousness is absent or judgment is being executed. Even though Yahweh established Israel as a nation to produce justice and righteousness, he discovered bloodshed and a cry; i.e., the city was oppressing the unfortunate (Isa 5:7). The righteous lament in loud cries over the loss suffered by their nation (cf. 33:7; Lam 2:18). They intercede for forgiveness by repenting of the sins which led to this calamity and seeking God's help for the future. God listens to the cries of men, particularly when the righteous cry out under affliction. The Hebrews cried under the weight of their bondage in Egypt (Ex 3:7). God heard their cry and came to deliver them through the mighty deeds at the Exodus. Because of the cry of the oppressed in Sodom and Gomorrah, God came to judge the oppressors (Gen 18:21; 19:13). God especially promises to hear the cry of the afflicted, the alien, the orphan, and the widow (Ex 22:22f. [H 21f.]; cf. Ps 9:12 [H 13]). The fact that God hears the cries of his people and delivers them from their distress distinguishes him as the true, living God; for men cry to idols, but they do not respond (107:6, 28; Isa 46:7).

God, however, returns punishment to the wicked in kind. In response to the outcry of the Hebrews, the Egyptians uttered a great cry because of their sorrow over the death of their firstborn (Ex 11:6; 12:30). In the end times a portion of the punishment of the wicked will be crying from a painful heart (Isa 65:14).

God's suffering servant accomplishes his task differently than earthly rulers who seek reform and office. He will not cry in the streets (42:2); i.e. he will not seek through rhetoric to arouse the multitudes to move against their present rulers.

In the Niphal and Hiphil צָעַק means "to be called into assembly" (cf. Jud 7:23f.). A leader may summon the people together to pursue their enemies. Saul was the first leader since the Conquest who was able to assemble the entire nation, to go to battle against their enemies (1 Sam 13:4). The people could also be called into assembly in order for their leaders to present an important matter, Samuel gathered such an assembly at Mizpah in order to install Saul as King (10:17). Bibliography: THAT, II, pp. 568–74."[26]

The absence of righteousness was because of the unfair economic conditions. In the chapter, Nehemiah said that people were charging usury fees. That is a sign of unrighteousness."[27]

---

[26] R. Laird Harris, Gleason L. Archer, and Bruce K. Waltke, *Theological Wordbook of the Old Testament* (Chicago: Moody Press, 2004).

2. 1088 לָוָה (lāwâ) II, borrow (Qal), lend (Hiphil). (v. 4)

"This may be a specialized usage of לָוָה (supra). In contrast to the purely economic significance of borrowing and lending in modern life, these acts were endowed with a special theological significance in the OT. Only once is borrowing referred to as a primarily economic act in the borrowing of the restored Hebrew community to raise money for paying taxes (Neh 5:4). Also, the borrower and the lender are once referred to as one of several pairs expressing all classes of society (Isa 24:2).

Remaining usages reflect the special theological and moral perspectives of the OT. The Hebrew was not permitted to receive interest for loaning to another Hebrew (Ex 22:24–25). [Another view (reflected in KJV) is that interest on loans was allowed but not excessive interest (usury). In defense of this position, E. A. Speiser shows that in the surrounding cultures a loan was discounted with interest paid in advance. The thing prohibited in Akkadian sources and in the biblical laws was additional interest after a defaulting debtor was enslaved. See the fuller discussion and refs. under נֶשֶׁךְ. R.L.H.] Willingness to lend was a sign of righteous graciousness (Ps 112:5). Sometimes, the expectation or obligation of concrete repayment may be so remote or inappropriate that "lending" becomes almost synonymous with "giving" (Prov 19:17; note also "loan" and "give" as parallel in Ps 37:26).

The want or poverty which leads to borrowing is said to indicate the absence of God's blessing (Deut 28:44), while the ability to grant a loan characterizes a God-given prosperity (28:12). Inability to repay debts shows the futility of the wicked

(Ps 37:21). Finally, Scripture observes that the borrower is a slave to the lender (Prov 22:7). Bibliography: "Loans "in JewEnc."[28]

10. לְמִדַּת הַמֶּלֶךְ (v. 4) – this phrase translates as "for the King's tax." This tax was a special tax levied upon estates. Many landowners had to borrow money from the King to pay this tax. The borrowed land became the King's land until the loan was repaid. Through the King's tax, these landowners did not have money to purchase food. The famine was brutal upon them.

Culture Section

Questioning the passage

1. Does verse five say "to borrow money" or "have borrowed money?"
    The Aramaic version of Nehemiah uses the word *Nezap*. This word means "to borrow." In the Near East, Kings would loan money to farmers during famines and disasters. Most of the time, the loans were repaid. A part of the produce from the farm would be given to the King to repay the loans. During a famine, Persian kings were very magnanimous toward their subjects and gave food freely.[29]

    The tense matters because if the people had borrowed the money from the King they were under contract to pay back the loan with produce. If the word is in the future tense, then the loan has not been established. Nehemiah wanted Judea to be able to stand alone. Borrowing money from the Persian King meant that the

---

[13] IBID.
[29] Rocco A. Errico and George M. Lamsa, *Aramaic Light on Ezra Through the Song of Solomon* (Smyrna, GA: Noohra Foundation, 2010).

people had developed a relationship of dependence. The newly formed nation would always be dependent on the Persian Empire if they took the King's loans.

2. Why were the priests called in to administer the oath? (v. 12)

It was the custom of the day to have the priests (Levites) administer all oaths. Ancient oaths were made in the name of the LORD. To break an oath would cause the person to be expelled from the community and shunned for the rest of their lives.

3. What does it mean to shake the front of a garment? (v. 13)

The garment is probably the *tallis* with the *tzitzit*. This garment is called a prayer cloth in English. The strings on the edges of the cloth represent the Word of the LORD, the Torah. When the oaths were made in the LORD's name, they were "sealed" by the *tzitzit*. This type of oath was considered unbreakable.

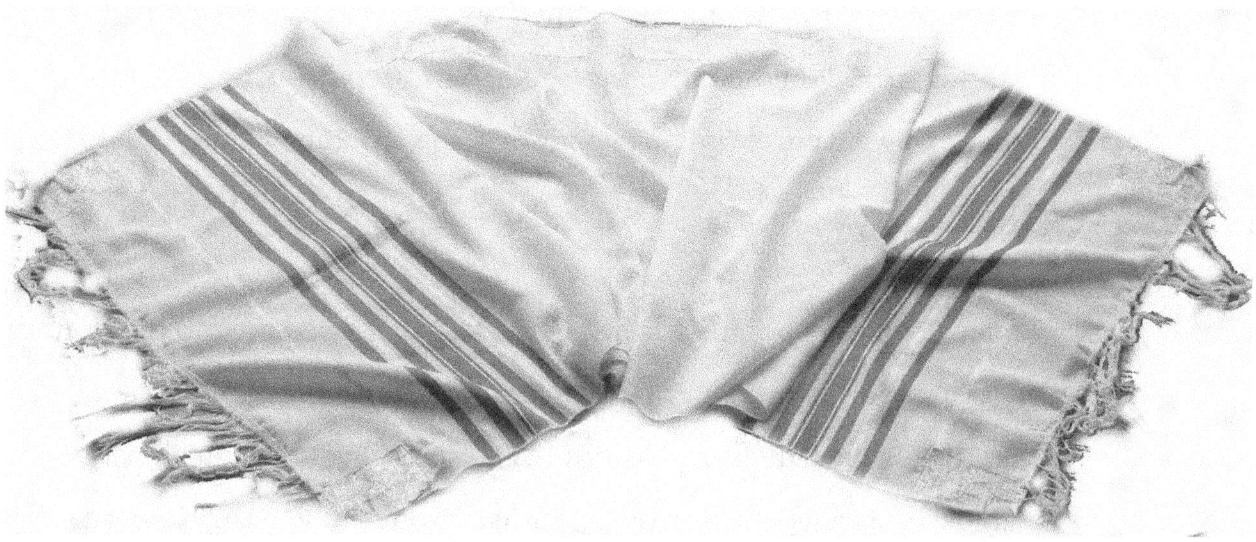

30

---

30 http://2.bp.blogspot.com/-HUBWTHv31Tw/UoADggnNWII/AAAAAAAAAzw/smMSVks8M5s/s1600/tallit.jpg

Thoughts

Nehemiah attempted to get Judea and Jerusalem independent from the King. He knew that the returning nation would always be a province of Persia. However, he could lessen the King's influence on the people if he made them self-sufficient. When people become dependent on a government, even their own, they become servants of the government. Freedom requires that people have little reliance on their government for their daily needs.

Chapter Six

Language

New American Standard 1995	**Hebrew**
Neh. 6:1 Now when it was reported to Sanballat, Tobiah, to Geshem the Arab and to the rest of our enemies that I had rebuilt the wall, and *that* no breach remained in it, [a]although at that time I had not set up the doors in the gates, 2 then Sanballat and Geshem sent *a message* to me, saying, "Come, let us meet together at [1]Chephirim in the plain of [a]Ono." But they were planning to [2]harm me. 3 So I sent messengers to them, saying, "I am doing a great work and I cannot come down. Why should the work stop while I leave it and come down to you?" 4 They sent *messages* to me four times in this manner, and I answered them in the same way. 5 Then Sanballat sent his servant to me in the same manner a fifth time with an open letter in his hand. 6 In it was written, "It is reported among the nations, and [1]Gashmu says, that [a]you and the Jews are planning to rebel; therefore you are rebuilding the wall. And you are to be their king, according to these reports. 7 "You have also appointed prophets to proclaim in Jerusalem concerning [1]you, 'A king is in Judah!' And now it will be reported to the king according to these reports. So come now, let us take counsel together." 8 Then I sent *a message* to him saying, "Such things as you are saying have not been done, but you are [a]inventing them [1]in your own mind." 9 For all of them were *trying* to	Neh. 6:1 וַיְהִ֣י כַאֲשֶׁ֣ר נִשְׁמַ֣ע לְסַנְבַלַּ֡ט וְטוֹבִיָּ֣ה וּלְגֶ֩שֶׁם֩ הָעַרְבִ֨י וּלְיֶ֜תֶר אֹֽיְבֵ֗ינוּ כִּ֤י בָנִ֙יתִי֙ אֶת־הַ֣חוֹמָ֔ה וְלֹא־נ֥וֹתַר בָּ֖הּ פָּ֑רֶץ גַּ֚ם עַד־הָעֵ֣ת הַהִ֔יא דְּלָת֕וֹת לֹא־הֶעֱמַ֖דְתִּי בַּשְּׁעָרִֽים׃ 2 וַיִּשְׁלַ֣ח סַנְבַלַּ֣ט וְ֠גֶשֶׁם אֵלַ֤י לֵאמֹר֙ לְכָ֞ה וְנִֽוָּעֲדָ֥ה יַחְדָּ֛ו בַּכְּפִירִ֖ים בְּבִקְעַ֣ת אוֹנ֑וֹ וְהֵ֙מָּה֙ חֹֽשְׁבִ֔ים לַעֲשׂ֥וֹת לִ֖י רָעָֽה׃ 3 וָאֶשְׁלְחָ֨ה עֲלֵיהֶ֤ם מַלְאָכִים֙ לֵאמֹ֔ר מְלָאכָ֤ה גְדוֹלָה֙ אֲנִ֣י עֹשֶׂ֔ה וְלֹ֥א אוּכַ֖ל לָרֶ֑דֶת לָ֣מָּה תִשְׁבַּ֤ת הַמְּלָאכָה֙ כַּאֲשֶׁ֣ר אַרְפֶּ֔הָ וְיָרַדְתִּ֖י אֲלֵיכֶֽם׃ 4 וַיִּשְׁלְח֥וּ אֵלַ֛י כַּדָּבָ֥ר הַזֶּ֖ה אַרְבַּ֣ע פְּעָמִ֑ים וָאָשִׁ֥יב אוֹתָ֖ם כַּדָּבָ֥ר הַזֶּֽה׃ ס 5 וַיִּשְׁלַח֩ אֵלַ֨י סַנְבַלַּ֜ט כַּדָּבָ֥ר הַזֶּ֛ה פַּ֥עַם חֲמִישִׁ֖ית אֶֽת־נַעֲר֑וֹ וְאִגֶּ֥רֶת פְּתוּחָ֖ה בְּיָדֽוֹ׃ 6 כָּת֣וּב בָּ֗הּ בַּגּוֹיִ֤ם נִשְׁמָע֙ וְגַשְׁמ֣וּ אֹמֵ֔ר אַתָּ֤ה וְהַיְּהוּדִים֙ חֹשְׁבִ֣ים לִמְר֔וֹד עַל־כֵּ֛ן אַתָּ֥ה בוֹנֶ֖ה הַחוֹמָ֑ה וְאַתָּ֗ה הֹוֶ֤ה לָהֶם֙ לְמֶ֔לֶךְ כַּדְּבָרִ֖ים הָאֵֽלֶּה׃ 7 וְגַם־נְבִיאִ֡ים הֶעֱמַ֣דְתָּ לִקְרֹא֩ עָלֶ֨יךָ בִֽירוּשָׁלַ֜͏ִם

frighten us, [1]thinking, "[2]They will become discouraged with the work and it will not be done." But now, [a]*O God,* strengthen my hands.

Neh. 6:10 When I entered the house of Shemaiah the son of Delaiah, son of Mehetabel, [a]who was [1]confined at home, he said, "Let us meet together in the house of God, within the temple, and let us close the doors of the temple, for they are coming to kill you, and they are coming to kill you at night." [11] But I said, "[a]Should a man like me flee? And could one such as I go into the temple [1]to save his life? I will not go in." [12] Then I perceived [1]that surely God had not sent him, but he uttered *his* prophecy against me because Tobiah and Sanballat had hired him. [13] He was hired for this reason, [a]that I might become frightened and act accordingly and sin, so that they might have an evil report in order that they could reproach me. [14] [a]Remember, O my God, Tobiah and Sanballat according to these works of theirs, and also Noadiah [b]the prophetess and the rest of the prophets who were *trying* to frighten me.

Neh. 6:15 So [a]the wall was completed on the twenty-fifth of *the month* Elul, in fifty-two days. [16] [a]When all our enemies heard *of it,* and all the nations surrounding us saw *it,* they [1]lost their confidence; for [b]they recognized that this work had been accomplished [2]with the help of our God. [17] Also in those days many letters went from the nobles of Judah to Tobiah, and Tobiah's *letters* came to them. [18] For many in Judah were bound by oath to him because he was the son-in-law of

לֵאמֹר מֶלֶךְ בִּיהוּדָה וְעַתָּה יִשָּׁמַע
לַמֶּלֶךְ כַּדְּבָרִים הָאֵלֶּה וְעַתָּה לְכָה
וְנִוָּעֲצָה יַחְדָּו ׃ ס [8] וָאֶשְׁלְחָה אֵלָיו
לֵאמֹר לֹא נִהְיָה כַּדְּבָרִים הָאֵלֶּה
אֲשֶׁר אַתָּה אוֹמֵר כִּי מִלִּבְּךָ אַתָּה
בוֹדָאם ׃ [9] כִּי כֻלָּם מְיָרְאִים אוֹתָנוּ
לֵאמֹר יִרְפּוּ יְדֵיהֶם מִן־הַמְּלָאכָה
וְלֹא תֵעָשֶׂה וְעַתָּה חַזֵּק אֶת־יָדָי ׃ [10]
וַאֲנִי־בָאתִי בֵּית שְׁמַעְיָה בֶן־דְּלָיָה
בֶּן־מְהֵיטַבְאֵל וְהוּא עָצוּר וַיֹּאמֶר
נִוָּעֵד אֶל־בֵּית הָאֱלֹהִים אֶל־תּוֹךְ
הַהֵיכָל וְנִסְגְּרָה דַּלְתוֹת הַהֵיכָל כִּי
בָּאִים לְהָרְגֶךָ וְלַיְלָה בָּאִים
לְהָרְגֶךָ ׃ [11] וָאֹמְרָה הַאִישׁ כָּמוֹנִי
יִבְרָח וּמִי כָמוֹנִי אֲשֶׁר־יָבוֹא אֶל־
הַהֵיכָל וָחָי לֹא אָבוֹא ׃ [12] וָאַכִּירָה
וְהִנֵּה לֹא־אֱלֹהִים שְׁלָחוֹ כִּי
הַנְּבוּאָה דִּבֶּר עָלַי וְטוֹבִיָּה
וְסַנְבַלַּט שְׂכָרוֹ ׃ [13] לְמַעַן שָׂכוּר הוּא
לְמַעַן־אִירָא וְאֶעֱשֶׂה־כֵּן וְחָטָאתִי
וְהָיָה לָהֶם לְשֵׁם רָע לְמַעַן
יְחָרְפוּנִי ׃ פ [14] זָכְרָה אֱלֹהַי לְטוֹבִיָּה
וּלְסַנְבַלַּט כְּמַעֲשָׂיו אֵלֶּה וְגַם
לְנוֹעַדְיָה הַנְּבִיאָה וּלְיֶתֶר הַנְּבִיאִים
אֲשֶׁר הָיוּ מְיָרְאִים אוֹתִי ׃ [15] וַתִּשְׁלַם
הַחוֹמָה בְּעֶשְׂרִים וַחֲמִשָּׁה לֶאֱלוּל
לַחֲמִשִּׁים וּשְׁנַיִם יוֹם ׃ פ [16] וַיְהִי
כַּאֲשֶׁר שָׁמְעוּ כָּל־אוֹיְבֵינוּ וַיִּרְאוּ

Shecaniah the son of Arah, and his son Jehohanan had married the daughter of Meshullam the son of Berechiah. **19** Moreover, they were speaking about his good deeds in my presence and reported my words to him. Then Tobiah sent letters to frighten me.

כָּל־הַגּוֹיִם֙ אֲשֶׁ֣ר סְבִיבֹתֵ֔ינוּ וַיִּפְּל֖וּ מְאֹ֣ד בְּעֵינֵיהֶ֑ם וַיֵּ֣דְע֔וּ כִּ֣י מֵאֵ֤ת אֱלֹהֵ֨ינוּ֙ נֶעֶשְׂתָ֔ה הַמְּלָאכָ֖ה הַזֹּֽאת׃ **17** גַּ֣ם ׀ בַּיָּמִ֣ים הָהֵ֗ם מַרְבִּ֞ים חֹרֵ֤י יְהוּדָה֙ אִגְּרֹ֣תֵיהֶ֔ם הוֹלְכ֖וֹת עַל־טוֹבִיָּ֑ה וַאֲשֶׁ֥ר לְטוֹבִיָּ֖ה בָּא֥וֹת אֲלֵיהֶֽם׃ **18** כִּי־רַבִּ֣ים בִּֽיהוּדָ֗ה בַּעֲלֵ֤י שְׁבוּעָה֙ ל֔וֹ כִּי־חָתָ֥ן ה֖וּא לִשְׁכַנְיָ֣ה בֶן־אָרַ֑ח וִיהוֹחָנָ֣ן בְּנ֔וֹ לָקַ֕ח אֶת־בַּת־מְשֻׁלָּ֖ם בֶּ֥ן בֶּרֶכְיָֽה׃ **19** גַּ֣ם טוֹבֹתָ֗יו הָי֤וּ אֹמְרִים֙ לְפָנַ֔י וּדְבָרַ֕י הָי֥וּ מוֹצִיאִ֖ים ל֑וֹ אִגְּר֛וֹת שָׁלַ֥ח טוֹבִיָּ֖ה לְיָֽרְאֵֽנִי׃

References

Nehemiah 6:1 [a]Neh 3:1, 3	**Nehemiah 6:10** [1]Lit *shut up* [a]Jer 36:5
Nehemiah 6:2 [1]Another reading is, one of *the villages* [2]Lit *do evil to me* [a]1 Chr 8:12	**Nehemiah 6:11** [1]Lit *and live* [a]Prov 28:1
Nehemiah 6:6 [1]In v 1 and elsewhere, *Geshem* [a]Neh 2:19	**Nehemiah 6:12** [1]Lit *and behold God*
Nehemiah 6:7 [1]Lit *you, saying*	**Nehemiah 6:13** [a]Neh 6:6
Nehemiah 6:8 [1]Lit *from your heart* [a]Job 13:4; Ps 52:2	**Nehemiah 6:14** [a]Neh 13:29 [b]Ezek 13:17
Nehemiah 6:9 [1]Lit *saying,* [2]Lit *Their hands will drop from* [a]Ps 138:3	**Nehemiah 6:15** [a]Neh 4:1, 2
	Nehemiah 6:16 [1]Lit *fell exceedingly in their own eyes* [2]Lit *from our God* [a]Neh 2:10; 4:1, 7 [b]Ex 14:25

Process of Discovery

Linguistics Section

Linguistic Structure

A [1]   Now when it was reported to Sanballat, Tobiah, to Geshem the Arab and to the rest of our enemies that I had rebuilt the wall, and *that* no breach remained in it, *a*although at that time I had not set up the doors in the gates, [2] then Sanballat and Geshem sent *a message* to me, saying, "Come, let us meet together at [1]Chephirim in the plain of *a*Ono." But they were planning to [2]harm me. [3] So I sent messengers to them, saying, "I am doing a great work and I cannot come down. Why should the work stop while I leave it and come down to you?" [4] They sent *messages* to me four times in this manner, and I answered them in the same way. [5] Then Sanballat sent his servant to me in the same manner a fifth time with an open letter in his hand. [6] In it was written, "It is reported among the nations, and [1]Gashmu says, that *a*you and the Jews are planning to rebel; therefore you are rebuilding the wall. And you are to be their king, according to these reports. [7] "You have also appointed prophets to proclaim in Jerusalem concerning [1]you, 'A king is in Judah!' And now it will be reported to the king according to these reports. So come now, let us take counsel together." [8] Then I sent *a message* to him saying, "Such things as you are saying have not been done, but you are *a*inventing them [1]in your own mind."

B [9] For all of them were *trying* to frighten us, [1]thinking, "[2]They will become discouraged with the work and it will not be done." But now, *a*O God, strengthen my hands.

C [10] When I entered the house of Shemaiah the son of Delaiah, son of Mehetabel, *a*who was [1]confined at home, he said, "Let us meet together in the house of God, within the temple, and let us close the doors of the temple, for they are coming to kill you, and they are coming to kill you at night." [11] But I said, "[a]Should a man like me flee? And could one such as I go into the temple [1]to save his life? I will not go in." [12] Then I perceived [1]that surely God had not sent him, but he uttered *his* prophecy against me because Tobiah and Sanballat had hired him. [13] He was hired for this reason, *a*that I might become frightened and act accordingly and sin, so that they might have an evil report in order that they could reproach me.

B' [14] *a*Remember, O my God, Tobiah and Sanballat according to these works of theirs, and also Noadiah *b*the prophetess and the rest of the prophets who were *trying* to frighten me.

A' [15]   So *ᵃthe wall was completed on the twenty-fifth of *the month* Elul, in fifty-two days. [16] *ᵃWhen all our enemies heard *of it,* and all the nations surrounding us saw *it,* they ¹lost their confidence; for *ᵇthey recognized that this work had been accomplished ²with the help of our God. [17] Also in those days many letters went from the nobles of Judah to Tobiah, and Tobiah's *letters* came to them. [18] For many in Judah were bound by oath to him because he was the son-in-law of Shecaniah the son of Arah, and his son Jehohanan had married the daughter of Meshullam the son of Berechiah. [19] Moreover, they were speaking about his good deeds in my presence and reported my words to him. Then Tobiah sent letters to frighten me.

A: Intimidation of enemies. B: Prayer of Nehemiah. C: False prophecy.[31]

Discussion

This chapter forms an A-B-C chiasm. The center of the chiasm is Nehemiah's prayer. The people who were against the rebuilding of the walls of Jerusalem feared that Nehemiah was going to attempt a rebellion against the Persian Empire. Nehemiah would have become the King of Jerusalem. This was a rumor fueled by disinformation about Nehemiah's intent. Nehemiah was the cupbearer to the King. He never intended or wanted Judea to break away from the Empire. Nehemiah knew in his heart that Judea would not have lasted long against the Persian Empire's army.

Questioning the Passage

1. What is the time period described in verse fifteen?

   It was the twentieth year of the reign of King Darius. This was the year Nehemiah arrived in Jerusalem. The wall was completed fifty-two days after Nehemiah got the work started. Nehemiah pushed for the completion of the wall because the enemies of the Jews were preparing to attack the city.

---

[31] Hajime Murai, "Literary Structure (Chiasm, Chiasmus) of Book of Ezra and Nehemiah," Literary structure (chiasm, chiasmus) of each pericopes of Book of Ezra and Nehemiah, accessed April 26, 2021, http://www.bible.literarystructure.info/bible/15_EzraNehemiah_pericope_e.html.

Biblical Personalities

1. Noadiah – "Our only source of information about the prophetess Noadiah is the book of Nehemiah. The book is the memoir of a governor appointed by the Persian king after the exile of the Israelite people in the 5th century B.C.E. He was not a prophet, priest or king and therefore had no mandate from the Jewish people or God. Artaxerxes I awarded him the task of rebuilding the walls of Jerusalem and continuing the restoration of the Temple."[32]

Biblical Locations

1. Chephririm

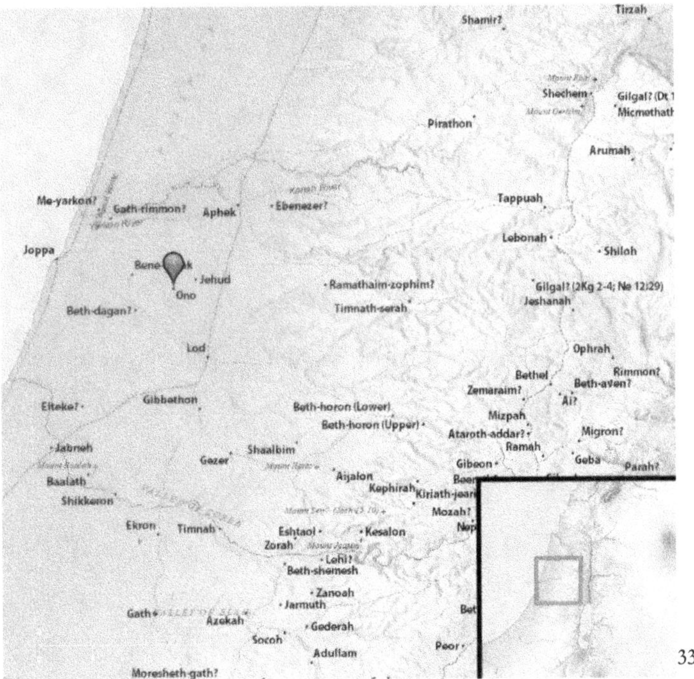

[33]

---

[32] Robin, "Noadiah: The Lost Prophetess," Robin Cohn, September 20, 2010, https://robincohn.net/noadiah-the-lost-prophetess/.

[33] Bible Map: Hakkephirim (Ono), accessed April 26, 2021, https://bibleatlas.org/full/hakkephirim.htm.

Thoughts

The Hebrew people have always had enemies that wanted to kill them. Even today, Israel has enemies that want to destroy the nation and wipe it off the face of the Earth. Throughout the centuries, the LORD has protected His people. No nation has or will ever destroy all of the Jewish race. The LORD has promised that a remnant of the people will always exist.

Thoughts

Chapter Seven

Language

New American Standard 1995	Hebrew
Neh. 7:1 Now when [a]the wall was rebuilt and I had set up the doors, and the gatekeepers and the singers and the Levites were appointed, [2] then I put [a]Hanani my brother, and [b]Hananiah the commander of [c]the fortress, in charge of Jerusalem, for he was [d]a faithful man and feared God more than many. [3] Then I said to them, "Do not let the gates of Jerusalem be opened until the sun is hot, and while they are standing *guard,* let them shut and bolt the doors. Also appoint guards from the inhabitants of Jerusalem, each at his post, and each in front of his own house." [4] Now the city was large and spacious, but the people in it were few and the houses were not built. **Neh. 7:5** [a]Then my God put it into my heart to assemble the nobles, the officials and the people to be enrolled by genealogies. Then I found the book of the genealogy of those who came up first [1]in which I found the following record: **Neh. 7:6** [a]These are the [1]people of the province who came up from the captivity of the exiles whom Nebuchadnezzar the king of Babylon had carried away, and who returned to Jerusalem and Judah, each to his city, [7] who came with Zerubbabel, Jeshua, Nehemiah, [1]Azariah,	Neh. 7:1 וַיְהִ֗י כַּאֲשֶׁ֤ר נִבְנְתָה֙ הַחוֹמָ֔ה וָאַעֲמִ֖יד הַדְּלָת֑וֹת וַיִּפָּ֣קְד֔וּ הַשּׁוֹעֲרִ֥ים וְהַמְשֹׁרְרִ֖ים וְהַלְוִיִּֽם׃ 2 וָאֲצַוֶּ֞ה אֶת־חֲנָ֣נִי אָחִ֗י וְאֶת־חֲנַנְיָ֛ה שַׂ֥ר הַבִּירָ֖ה עַל־יְרוּשָׁלָ֑͏ִם כִּי־הוּא֙ כְּאִ֣ישׁ אֱמֶ֔ת וְיָרֵ֥א אֶת־הָאֱלֹהִ֖ים מֵרַבִּֽים׃ 3 וַיֹּאמֶר [וָ][אֹמַר] לָהֶ֗ם לֹ֣א יִפָּֽתְחוּ֩ שַׁעֲרֵ֨י יְרוּשָׁלַ֜͏ִם עַד־חֹ֣ם הַשֶּׁ֗מֶשׁ וְעַ֣ד הֵ֤ם עֹמְדִים֙ יָגִ֣יפוּ הַדְּלָת֔וֹת וֶאֱחֹ֑זוּ וְהַעֲמֵ֗יד מִשְׁמְרוֹת֙ יֹשְׁבֵ֣י יְרוּשָׁלַ֔͏ִם אִ֤ישׁ בְּמִשְׁמָרוֹ֙ וְאִ֖ישׁ נֶ֥גֶד בֵּיתֽוֹ׃ 4 וְהָעִ֞יר רַחֲבַ֤ת יָדַ֙יִם֙ וּגְדוֹלָ֔ה וְהָעָ֥ם מְעַ֖ט בְּתוֹכָ֑הּ וְאֵ֥ין בָּתִּ֖ים בְּנוּיִֽם׃ 5 וַיִּתֵּ֤ן אֱלֹהַי֙ אֶל־לִבִּ֔י וָאֶקְבְּצָ֞ה אֶת־הַחֹרִ֧ים וְאֶת־הַסְּגָנִ֛ים וְאֶת־הָעָ֖ם לְהִתְיַחֵ֑שׂ וָֽאֶמְצָ֗א סֵ֤פֶר הַיַּ֙חַשׂ֙ הָעוֹלִ֣ים בָּרִאשׁוֹנָ֔ה וָאֶמְצָ֖א כָּת֥וּב בּֽוֹ׃ פ 6 אֵ֣לֶּה ׀ בְּנֵ֣י הַמְּדִינָ֗ה הָעֹלִים֙ מִשְּׁבִ֣י הַגּוֹלָ֔ה אֲשֶׁ֣ר הֶגְלָ֔ה נְבוּכַדְנֶצַּ֖ר מֶ֣לֶךְ בָּבֶ֑ל וַיָּשׁ֧וּבוּ לִירֽוּשָׁלַ֛͏ִם וְלִיהוּדָ֖ה אִ֥ישׁ לְעִירֽוֹ׃ 7 הַבָּאִ֣ים עִם־זְרֻבָּבֶ֗ל יֵשׁ֡וּעַ נְחֶמְיָ֡ה עֲ֠זַרְיָ֠ה רַֽעַמְיָ֨ה נַחֲמָ֜נִי מָרְדֳּכַ֥י בִּלְשָׁ֛ן מִסְפֶּ֥רֶת בִּגְוַ֖י נְח֣וּם בַּעֲנָ֑ה מִסְפַּ֕ר אַנְשֵׁ֖י עַ֥ם יִשְׂרָאֵֽל׃ ס 8 בְּנֵ֣י פַרְעֹ֔שׁ אַלְפַּ֕יִם מֵאָ֖ה וְשִׁבְעִ֥ים וּשְׁנָֽיִם׃ ס 9 בְּנֵ֣י שְׁפַטְיָ֔ה שְׁלֹ֥שׁ מֵא֖וֹת שִׁבְעִ֥ים וּשְׁנָֽיִם׃ ס 10 בְּנֵ֣י אָרַ֔ח שֵׁ֥שׁ מֵא֖וֹת חֲמִשִּׁ֥ים וּשְׁנָֽיִם׃ ס 11 בְּנֵֽי־פַחַ֥ת מוֹאָ֛ב לִבְנֵ֥י יֵשׁ֖וּעַ וְיוֹאָ֑ב אַלְפַּ֕יִם וּשְׁמֹנֶ֥ה מֵא֖וֹת שְׁמֹנָ֥ה עָשָֽׂר׃ ס 12 בְּנֵ֣י עֵילָ֔ם אֶ֕לֶף מָאתַ֖יִם חֲמִשִּׁ֥ים וְאַרְבָּעָֽה׃ ס 13 בְּנֵ֣י זַתּ֔וּא שְׁמֹנֶ֥ה מֵא֖וֹת אַרְבָּעִ֥ים וַחֲמִשָּֽׁה׃ ס 14 בְּנֵ֣י זַכָּ֔י שְׁבַ֥ע מֵא֖וֹת וְשִׁשִּֽׁים׃ ס 15 בְּנֵ֣י בִנּ֔וּי שֵׁ֥שׁ מֵא֖וֹת

[2]Raamiah, Nahamani, Mordecai, Bilshan, [3]Mispereth, Bigvai, [4]Nehum, Baanah.

The number of men of the people of Israel: [8] the sons of Parosh, 2,172; [9] the sons of Shephatiah, 372; [10] the sons of Arah, 652; [11] the sons of Pahath-moab of the sons of Jeshua and Joab, 2,818; [12] the sons of Elam, 1,254; [13] the sons of Zattu, 845; [14] the sons of Zaccai, 760; [15] the sons of [1]Binnui, 648; [16] the sons of Bebai, 628; [17] the sons of Azgad, 2,322; [18] the sons of Adonikam, 667; [19] the sons of Bigvai, 2,067; [20] the sons of Adin, 655; [21] the sons of Ater, of Hezekiah, 98; [22] the sons of Hashum, 328; [23] the sons of Bezai, 324; [24] the sons of [1]Hariph, 112; [25] the sons of [1]Gibeon, 95; [26] the men of Bethlehem and Netophah, 188; [27] the men of Anathoth, 128; [28] the men of [1]Beth-azmaveth, 42; [29] the men of [1]Kiriath-jearim, Chephirah and Beeroth, 743; [30] the men of Ramah and Geba, 621; [31] the men of Michmas, 122; [32] the men of Bethel and Ai, 123; [33] the men of the other Nebo, 52; [34] the sons of the other Elam, 1,254; [35] the sons of Harim, 320; [36] the [1]men of Jericho, 345; [37] the sons of Lod, Hadid and Ono, 721; [38] the sons of Senaah, 3,930.

Neh. 7:39   The priests: the sons of Jedaiah of the house of Jeshua, 973; [40] the sons of Immer, 1,052; [41] the sons of Pashhur, 1,247; [42] the sons of Harim, 1,017.

Neh. 7:43   The Levites: the sons of Jeshua, of Kadmiel, of the sons of [1]Hodevah, 74. [44] The singers: the sons of Asaph, 148. [45] The gatekeepers: the sons of Shallum, the sons of Ater, the sons of

16 ס : בְּנֵי בֵבָי שֵׁשׁ מֵאוֹת אַרְבָּעִים וּשְׁמֹנָה :

17 ס : בְּנֵי עַזְגָּד אַלְפַּיִם שְׁלֹשׁ עֶשְׂרִים וּשְׁמֹנָה :

18 ס : בְּנֵי אֲדֹנִיקָם שֵׁשׁ מֵאוֹת עֶשְׂרִים וּשְׁנָיִם :

19 ס : בְּנֵי בִגְוָי אַלְפַּיִם מֵאוֹת שִׁשִּׁים וְשִׁבְעָה :

20 ס : בְּנֵי עָדִין שֵׁשׁ מֵאוֹת שִׁשִּׁים וְחָמִשָּׁה :

21 ס : בְּנֵי־אָטֵר לְחִזְקִיָּה חֲמִשִּׁים וַחֲמִשָּׁה :

22 ס : בְּנֵי חָשֻׁם שְׁלֹשׁ מֵאוֹת תִּשְׁעִים וּשְׁמֹנָה :

23 ס : בְּנֵי בֵצָי שְׁלֹשׁ מֵאוֹת עֶשְׂרִים וְאַרְבָּעָה :

24 ס : בְּנֵי חָרִיף מֵאָה שְׁנֵים עָשָׂר :

25 ס : בְּנֵי גִבְעוֹן תִּשְׁעִים וַחֲמִשָּׁה : ס 26

אַנְשֵׁי בֵית־לֶחֶם וּנְטֹפָה מֵאָה שְׁמֹנִים וּשְׁמֹנָה :

27 ס אַנְשֵׁי עֲנָתוֹת מֵאָה עֶשְׂרִים וּשְׁמֹנָה : ס 28

אַנְשֵׁי בֵית־עַזְמָוֶת אַרְבָּעִים וּשְׁנָיִם : ס 29

אַנְשֵׁי קִרְיַת יְעָרִים כְּפִירָה וּבְאֵרוֹת שְׁבַע מֵאוֹת אַרְבָּעִים וּשְׁלֹשָׁה : ס 30 אַנְשֵׁי הָרָמָה

וָגֶבַע שֵׁשׁ מֵאוֹת עֶשְׂרִים וְאֶחָד : ס 31 אַנְשֵׁי

מִכְמָס מֵאָה וְעֶשְׂרִים וּשְׁנָיִם : ס 32 אַנְשֵׁי

בֵית־אֵל וְהָעָי מֵאָה עֶשְׂרִים וּשְׁלֹשָׁה : ס 33

אַנְשֵׁי נְבוֹ אַחֵר חֲמִשִּׁים וּשְׁנָיִם : ס 34 בְּנֵי

עֵילָם אַחֵר אֶלֶף מָאתַיִם חֲמִשִּׁים וְאַרְבָּעָה :

35 ס בְּנֵי חָרִם שְׁלֹשׁ מֵאוֹת וְעֶשְׂרִים : ס 36 בְּנֵי

יְרֵחוֹ שְׁלֹשׁ מֵאוֹת אַרְבָּעִים וַחֲמִשָּׁה : ס 37

בְּנֵי־לֹד חָדִיד וְאוֹנוֹ שְׁבַע מֵאוֹת וְעֶשְׂרִים

וְאֶחָד : ס 38 בְּנֵי סְנָאָה שְׁלֹשֶׁת אֲלָפִים תְּשַׁע

מֵאוֹת וּשְׁלֹשִׁים : פ 39 הַכֹּהֲנִים בְּנֵי יְדַעְיָה

לְבֵית יֵשׁוּעַ תְּשַׁע מֵאוֹת שִׁבְעִים וּשְׁלֹשָׁה : ס

40 בְּנֵי אִמֵּר אֶלֶף חֲמִשִּׁים וּשְׁנָיִם : ס 41 בְּנֵי

פַשְׁחוּר אֶלֶף מָאתַיִם אַרְבָּעִים וְשִׁבְעָה : ס 42

בְּנֵי חָרִם אֶלֶף שִׁבְעָה עָשָׂר : פ 43 הַלְוִיִּם

בְּנֵי־יֵשׁוּעַ לְקַדְמִיאֵל לִבְנֵי לְהוֹדְוָה שִׁבְעִים

וְאַרְבָּעָה : ס 44 הַמְשֹׁרְרִים בְּנֵי אָסָף מֵאָה

אַרְבָּעִים וּשְׁמֹנָה : ס 45 הַשֹּׁעֲרִים בְּנֵי־שַׁלּוּם

בְּנֵי־אָטֵר בְּנֵי־טַלְמֹן בְּנֵי־עַקּוּב בְּנֵי חֲטִיטָא

Talmon, the sons of Akkub, the sons of Hatita, the sons of Shobai, 138.

Neh. 7:46 The temple servants: the sons of Ziha, the sons of Hasupha, the sons of Tabbaoth, [47] the sons of Keros, the sons of [1]Sia, the sons of Padon, [48] the sons of Lebana, the sons of Hagaba, the sons of Shalmai, [49] the sons of Hanan, the sons of Giddel, the sons of Gahar, [50] the sons of Reaiah, the sons of Rezin, the sons of Nekoda, [51] the sons of Gazzam, the sons of Uzza, the sons of Paseah, [52] the sons of Besai, the sons of Meunim, the sons of [1]Nephushesim, [53] the sons of Bakbuk, the sons of Hakupha, the sons of Harhur, [54] the sons of [1]Bazlith, the sons of Mehida, the sons of Harsha, [55] the sons of Barkos, the sons of Sisera, the sons of Temah, [56] the sons of Neziah, the sons of Hatipha.

Neh. 7:57 The sons of Solomon's servants: the sons of Sotai, the sons of [1]Sophereth, the sons of [2]Perida, [58] the sons of Jaala, the sons of Darkon, the sons of Giddel, [59] the sons of Shephatiah, the sons of Hattil, the sons of Pochereth-hazzebaim, the sons of [1]Amon.

Neh. 7:60 All the temple servants and the sons of Solomon's servants *were* 392.

Neh. 7:61 These *were* they who came up from Tel-melah, Tel-harsha, Cherub, [1]Addon and Immer; but they could not show their fathers' houses or their [2]descendants, whether they were of Israel: [62] the sons of Delaiah, the sons of Tobiah, the sons of Nekoda, 642. [63] Of the priests: the sons of [1]Hobaiah, the sons of

בְּנֵי שֹׁבָי מֵאָה שְׁלֹשִׁים וּשְׁמֹנָה ׃ ס [46] הַנְּתִינִים בְּנֵי־צִחָא בְנֵי־חֲשֻׂפָא בְּנֵי טַבָּעוֹת ׃ [47] בְּנֵי־קֵירֹס בְּנֵי־סִיעָא בְּנֵי פָדוֹן ׃ [48] בְּנֵי־לְבָנָה בְנֵי־חֲגָבָה בְּנֵי שַׁלְמָי ׃ [49] בְּנֵי־חָנָן בְּנֵי־גִדֵּל בְּנֵי־גָחַר ׃ [50] בְּנֵי־רְאָיָה בְנֵי־רְצִין בְּנֵי נְקוֹדָא ׃ [51] בְּנֵי־גַזָּם בְּנֵי־עֻזָּא בְּנֵי פָסֵחַ ׃ [52] בְּנֵי־בֵסַי בְּנֵי־מְעוּנִים בְּנֵי נְפוּשְׁסִים [נְפִישְׁסִים׃] [53] בְּנֵי־בַקְבּוּק בְּנֵי־חֲקוּפָא בְּנֵי חַרְחוּר ׃ [54] בְּנֵי־בַצְלִית בְּנֵי־מְחִידָא בְּנֵי חַרְשָׁא ׃ [55] בְּנֵי־בַרְקוֹס בְּנֵי־סִיסְרָא בְּנֵי־תָמַח ׃ [56] בְּנֵי נְצִיחַ בְּנֵי חֲטִיפָא ׃ [57] בְּנֵי עַבְדֵי שְׁלֹמֹה בְּנֵי־סוֹטַי בְּנֵי־סוֹפֶרֶת בְּנֵי פְרִידָא ׃ [58] בְּנֵי־יַעְלָא בְנֵי־דַרְקוֹן בְּנֵי גִדֵּל ׃ [59] בְּנֵי שְׁפַטְיָה בְנֵי־חַטִּיל בְּנֵי פֹכֶרֶת הַצְּבָיִים בְּנֵי אָמוֹן ׃ [60] כָּל־הַנְּתִינִים וּבְנֵי עַבְדֵי שְׁלֹמֹה שְׁלֹשׁ מֵאוֹת תִּשְׁעִים וּשְׁנָיִם ׃ פ [61] וְאֵלֶּה הָעוֹלִים מִתֵּל מֶלַח תֵּל חַרְשָׁא כְּרוּב אַדּוֹן וְאִמֵּר וְלֹא יָכְלוּ לְהַגִּיד בֵּית־אֲבוֹתָם וְזַרְעָם אִם מִיִּשְׂרָאֵל הֵם ׃ [62] בְּנֵי־דְלָיָה בְנֵי־טוֹבִיָּה בְּנֵי נְקוֹדָא שֵׁשׁ מֵאוֹת וְאַרְבָּעִים וּשְׁנָיִם ׃ ס [63] וּמִן הַכֹּהֲנִים בְּנֵי חֳבַיָּה בְּנֵי הַקּוֹץ בְּנֵי בַרְזִלַּי אֲשֶׁר לָקַח מִבְּנוֹת בַּרְזִלַּי הַגִּלְעָדִי אִשָּׁה וַיִּקָּרֵא עַל־שְׁמָם ׃ [64] אֵלֶּה בִּקְשׁוּ כְתָבָם הַמִּתְיַחְשִׂים וְלֹא נִמְצָא וַיְגֹאֲלוּ מִן הַכְּהֻנָּה ׃ [65] וַיֹּאמֶר הַתִּרְשָׁתָא לָהֶם אֲשֶׁר לֹא־יֹאכְלוּ מִקֹּדֶשׁ הַקֳּדָשִׁים עַד עֲמֹד הַכֹּהֵן לְאוּרִים וְתוּמִּים ׃ [66] כָּל־הַקָּהָל כְּאֶחָד אַרְבַּע רִבּוֹא אַלְפַּיִם שְׁלֹשׁ־מֵאוֹת וְשִׁשִּׁים ׃ [67] מִלְּבַד עַבְדֵיהֶם וְאַמְהֹתֵיהֶם אֵלֶּה שִׁבְעַת אֲלָפִים שְׁלֹשׁ מֵאוֹת שְׁלֹשִׁים וְשִׁבְעָה וְלָהֶם מְשֹׁרְרִים וּמְשֹׁרְרוֹת מָאתַיִם וְאַרְבָּעִים וַחֲמִשָּׁה ׃ ס --

Hakkoz, the sons of Barzillai, who took a wife of the daughters of Barzillai, the Gileadite, and was named after them. [64] These searched *among* their ancestral registration, but it could not be located; therefore they were considered unclean *and excluded* from the priesthood. [65] [a]The [1]governor said to them that they should not eat from the most holy things until a priest arose with [b]Urim and Thummim.

Neh. 7:66 The whole assembly together *was* 42,360, [67] besides their male and their female servants, [1]of whom *there were* 7,337; and they had 245 male and female singers. [68] [1a]Their horses were 736; their mules, 245; [69] *their* camels, 435; *their* donkeys, 6,720.

Neh. 7:70 Some from among the heads of fathers' *households* gave to the work. The [1a]governor gave to the treasury 1,000 gold drachmas, 50 basins, 530 priests' garments. [71] Some of the heads of fathers' *households* gave into the treasury of the work 20,000 gold drachmas and 2,200 silver minas. [72] That which the rest of the people gave was 20,000 gold drachmas and 2,000 silver minas and 67 priests' garments.

Neh. 7:73 Now [a]the priests, the Levites, the gatekeepers, the singers, some of the people, the temple servants and all Israel, lived in their cities.

גְּמַלִּים אַרְבַּע מֵאֹות שְׁלֹשִׁים וַחֲמִשָּׁה ס 68 חֲמֹרִים שֵׁשֶׁת אֲלָפִים שְׁבַע מֵאֹות וְעֶשְׂרִים: 69 וּמִקְצָת רָאשֵׁי הָאָבֹות נָתְנוּ לַמְּלָאכָה הַתִּרְשָׁתָא נָתַן לָאֹוצָר זָהָב דַּרְכְּמֹנִים אֶלֶף מִזְרָקֹות חֲמִשִּׁים כָּתְנֹות כֹּהֲנִים שְׁלֹשִׁים וַחֲמֵשׁ מֵאֹות: 70 וּמֵרָאשֵׁי הָאָבֹות נָתְנוּ לְאֹוצַר הַמְּלָאכָה זָהָב דַּרְכְּמֹונִים שְׁתֵּי רִבֹּות וְכֶסֶף מָנִים אַלְפַּיִם וּמָאתָיִם: 71 וַאֲשֶׁר נָתְנוּ שְׁאֵרִית הָעָם זָהָב דַּרְכְּמֹונִים שְׁתֵּי רִבֹּוא וְכֶסֶף מָנִים אַלְפָּיִם וְכָתְנֹת כֹּהֲנִים שִׁשִּׁים וְשִׁבְעָה: פ 72 וַיֵּשְׁבוּ הַכֹּהֲנִים וְהַלְוִיִּם וְהַשֹּׁועֲרִים וְהַמְשֹׁרְרִים וּמִן הָעָם וְהַנְּתִינִים וְכָל יִשְׂרָאֵל בְּעָרֵיהֶם וַיִּגַּע הַחֹדֶשׁ הַשְּׁבִיעִי וּבְנֵי יִשְׂרָאֵל בְּעָרֵיהֶם:

References

Nehemiah 7:1
[a]Neh 6:1, 15

Nehemiah 7:2
[a]Neh 1:2
[b]Neh 10:23
[c]Neh 2:8
[d]Neh 13:13

Nehemiah 7:5
[1]Lit *and I found written in it*
[a]Prov 2:6; 3:6

Nehemiah 7:6
[1]Lit *sons*
[a]Ezra 2:1-70

Nehemiah 7:7
[1]In Ezra 2:2, *Seraiah*
[2]In Ezra 2:2, *Reelaiah*
[3]In Ezra 2:2, *Mispar*
[4]In Ezra 2:2, *Rehum*

Nehemiah 7:15
[1]In Ezra 2:10, *Bani*

Nehemiah 7:24
[1]In Ezra 2:18, *Jorah*

Nehemiah 7:25
[1]In Ezra 2:20, *Gibbar*

Nehemiah 7:28
[1]In Ezra 2:24, *Azmaveth*

Nehemiah 7:29
[1]In Ezra 2:25, *Kiriath-arim*

Nehemiah 7:36
[1]Lit *sons*

Nehemiah 7:43
[1]In Ezra 2:40, *Hodaviah*

Nehemiah 7:47
[1]In Ezra 2:44, *Siaha*

Nehemiah 7:52
[1]In Ezra 2:50, *Nephisim*

Nehemiah 7:54
[1]In Ezra 2:52, *Bazluth*

Nehemiah 7:57
[1]In Ezra 2:55, *Hassophereth*
[2]In Ezra 2:55, *Peruda*

Nehemiah 7:59
[1]In Ezra 2:57, *Ami*

Nehemiah 7:61
[1]In Ezra 2:59, *Addan*
[2]Lit *seed*

Nehemiah 7:63
[1]In Ezra 2:61, *Habaiah*

Nehemiah 7:65
[1]Heb *Tirshatha*, a Persian title
[a]Neh 8:9; 10:1
[b]Ex 28:30; Deut 33:8

Nehemiah 7:67
[1]Lit *these*

	Nehemiah 7:68 [1]So with some ancient mss and Gr [a]Ezra 2:66 **Nehemiah 7:70** [1]Heb *Tirshatha,* a Persian title [a]Neh 7:65; 8:9 **Nehemiah 7:73** [a]1 Chr 9:2 [b]Ezra 3:1

Process of Discovery

  Linguistics Section

    Linguistic Structure

  Discussion

  This chapter is a complete list of names of the aristocrats and nobles who returned to Jerusalem from Babylon. They created a book of lineage.

Chapter Eight

Language

New American Standard 1995	Hebrew
Neh. 8:1 And all the people gathered as one man at the square which was in front of [a]the Water Gate, and they [1]asked [b]Ezra the scribe to bring [c]the book of the law of Moses which the LORD had [2]given to Israel. [2] Then [a]Ezra the priest brought the law before the assembly of men, women and all who *could* listen with understanding, on [b]the first day of the seventh month. [3] He read from it before the square which was in front of [a]the Water Gate from [1]early morning until midday, in the presence of men and women, those who could understand; and all the people were attentive to the book of the law. [4] Ezra the scribe stood at a wooden podium which they had made for the purpose. And beside him stood Mattithiah, Shema, Anaiah, Uriah, Hilkiah, and Maaseiah on his right hand; and Pedaiah, Mishael, Malchijah, Hashum, Hashbaddanah, Zechariah *and* Meshullam on his left hand. [5] Ezra opened [a]the book in the sight of all the people for he was standing above all the people; and when he opened it, all the people [b]stood up. [6] Then Ezra blessed the LORD the great God. And all the people answered, "[a]Amen, Amen!" while lifting up their hands; then [b]they bowed low and worshiped the LORD with *their* faces to the ground. [7] Also Jeshua, Bani, Sherebiah, Jamin, Akkub, Shabbethai,	וַיֵּאָסְפ֤וּ כָל־הָעָם֙ כְּאִ֣ישׁ אֶחָ֔ד אֶל־ 1 הָ֣רְח֔וֹב אֲשֶׁ֖ר לִפְנֵ֣י שַֽׁעַר־הַמָּ֑יִם וַיֹּֽאמְרוּ֙ לְעֶזְרָ֣א הַסֹּפֵ֔ר לְהָבִ֕יא אֶת־סֵ֖פֶר תּוֹרַ֣ת מֹשֶׁ֔ה אֲשֶׁר־צִוָּ֥ה יְהוָ֖ה אֶת־יִשְׂרָאֵֽל׃ [2] וַיָּבִ֣יא עֶזְרָ֣א הַ֠כֹּהֵן אֶֽת־הַתּוֹרָ֞ה לִפְנֵ֤י הַקָּהָל֙ מֵאִ֣ישׁ וְעַד־אִשָּׁ֔ה וְכֹ֖ל מֵבִ֣ין לִשְׁמֹ֑עַ בְּי֥וֹם אֶחָ֖ד לַחֹ֥דֶשׁ הַשְּׁבִיעִֽי׃ [3] וַיִּקְרָא־בוֹ֩ לִפְנֵ֨י הָרְח֜וֹב אֲשֶׁ֣ר ׀ לִפְנֵ֣י שַֽׁעַר־הַמַּ֗יִם מִן־הָאוֹר֙ עַד־מַחֲצִ֣ית הַיּ֔וֹם נֶ֛גֶד הָאֲנָשִׁ֥ים וְהַנָּשִׁ֖ים וְהַמְּבִינִ֑ים וְאָזְנֵ֥י [4] כָל־הָעָ֖ם אֶל־סֵ֥פֶר הַתּוֹרָֽה׃ וַֽיַּעֲמֹ֞ד עֶזְרָ֣א הַסֹּפֵ֗ר עַֽל־מִגְדַּל־עֵץ֮ אֲשֶׁ֣ר עָשׂ֣וּ לַדָּבָר֒ וַיַּֽעֲמֹ֣ד אֶצְל֡וֹ מַתִּתְיָ֣ה וְשֶׁ֡מַע וַ֠עֲנָיָה וְאוּרִיָּ֧ה וְחִלְקִיָּ֛ה וּמַעֲשֵׂיָ֖ה עַל־ יְמִינ֑וֹ וּמִשְּׂמֹאל֗וֹ פְּ֠דָיָה וּמִֽישָׁאֵ֧ל וּמַלְכִּיָּ֛ה וְחָשֻׁ֥ם וְחַשְׁבַּדָּ֖נָה זְכַרְיָ֥ה [5] מְשֻׁלָּֽם׃ פ וַיִּפְתַּ֨ח עֶזְרָ֤א הַסֵּ֨פֶר֙ לְעֵינֵ֣י כָל־הָעָ֔ם כִּֽי־מֵעַ֥ל כָּל־הָעָ֖ם הָיָ֑ה וּכְפִתְח֖וֹ עָֽמְד֥וּ כָל־הָעָֽם׃ [6] וַיְבָ֣רֶךְ עֶזְרָ֔א אֶת־יְהוָ֥ה הָאֱלֹהִ֖ים הַגָּד֑וֹל וַיַּֽעֲנ֨וּ כָל־הָעָ֜ם אָמֵ֤ן ׀ אָמֵן֙ בְּמֹ֣עַל יְדֵיהֶ֔ם וַיִּקְּד֧וּ וַיִּשְׁתַּחֲוֻ֛ לַיהוָ֖ה אַפַּ֥יִם אָֽרְצָה׃ [7] וְיֵשׁ֡וּעַ וּבָנִ֡י וְשֵׁרֵ֥בְיָ֣ה ׀ יָמִ֣ין עַקּ֗וּב שַׁבְּתַ֣י ׀ הֽוֹדִיָּ֞ה מַעֲשֵׂיָ֧ה קְלִיטָ֛א עֲזַרְיָ֥ה יוֹזָבָ֖ד חָנָ֣ן פְּלָאיָ֑ה וְהַלְוִיִּ֔ם מְבִינִ֥ים אֶת־הָעָ֖ם [8] לַתּוֹרָ֑ה וְהָעָ֖ם עַל־עָמְדָֽם׃

Hodiah, Maaseiah, Kelita, Azariah, Jozabad, Hanan, Pelaiah, the Levites, explained the law to the people while the people *remained* in their place. [8] They read from the book, from the law of God, [1]translating to give the sense so that they understood the reading.

Neh. 8:9 Then Nehemiah, who was the [1a]governor, and Ezra [b]the priest *and* scribe, and the Levites who taught the people said to all the people, "This day is holy to the LORD your God; [d]do not mourn or weep." For all the people were weeping when they heard the words of the law. [10] Then he said to them, "Go, eat of the fat, drink of the sweet, and [a]send portions to him who has nothing prepared; for this day is holy to our Lord. Do not be grieved, for the joy of the LORD is your strength." [11] So the Levites calmed all the people, saying, "Be still, for the day is holy; do not be grieved." [12] All the people went away to eat, to drink, [a]to send portions and to [1]celebrate a great festival, [b]because they understood the words which had been made known to them.

Neh. 8:13 Then on the second day the heads of fathers' *households* of all the people, the priests and the Levites were gathered to Ezra the scribe that they might gain insight into the words of the law. [14] They found written in the law how the LORD had commanded through Moses that the sons of Israel [a]should live in booths during the feast of the seventh month. [15] [1a]So they proclaimed and circulated a proclamation in all their cities and [b]in Jerusalem, saying, "Go out to the

בַּסֵּ֖פֶר בְּתוֹרַ֣ת הָאֱלֹהִ֑ים מְפֹרָ֖שׁ וְשׂ֣וֹם שֶׂ֔כֶל וַיָּבִ֖ינוּ בַּמִּקְרָֽא׃ ס ⁹וַיֹּ֣אמֶר

נְחֶמְיָ֣ה ה֣וּא הַתִּרְשָׁ֡תָא וְעֶזְרָ֣א הַכֹּהֵ֣ן ׀ הַסֹּפֵ֡ר וְהַלְוִיִּם֩ הַמְּבִינִ֨ים אֶת־הָעָ֜ם לְכָל־הָעָ֗ם הַיּ֤וֹם קָדֹֽשׁ־הוּא֙ לַיהוָ֣ה אֱלֹֽהֵיכֶ֔ם אַל־תִּֽתְאַבְּל֖וּ וְאַל־תִּבְכּ֑וּ כִּ֤י בוֹכִים֙ כָּל־הָעָ֔ם כְּשָׁמְעָ֖ם אֶת־דִּבְרֵ֥י הַתּוֹרָֽה׃ ¹⁰וַיֹּ֣אמֶר לָהֶ֡ם לְכוּ֩ אִכְל֨וּ מַשְׁמַנִּ֜ים וּשְׁת֣וּ מַֽמְתַקִּ֗ים וְשִׁלְח֤וּ מָנוֹת֙ לְאֵ֣ין נָכ֣וֹן ל֔וֹ כִּֽי־קָד֥וֹשׁ הַיּ֖וֹם לַאֲדֹנֵ֑ינוּ וְאַל־תֵּ֣עָצֵ֔בוּ כִּֽי־חֶדְוַ֥ת יְהוָ֖ה הִ֥יא מָֽעֻזְּכֶֽם׃ ¹¹וְהַלְוִיִּ֞ם מַחְשִׁ֣ים לְכָל־הָעָ֗ם לֵאמֹ֥ר הַ֛סּוּ כִּ֥י הַיּ֖וֹם קָדֹ֑שׁ וְאַל־תֵּעָצֵֽבוּ׃ ¹²וַיֵּלְכ֨וּ כָל־הָעָ֜ם לֶאֱכֹ֤ל וְלִשְׁתּוֹת֙ וּלְשַׁלַּ֣ח מָנ֔וֹת וְלַעֲשׂ֖וֹת שִׂמְחָ֣ה גְדוֹלָ֑ה כִּ֤י הֵבִ֨ינוּ֙ בַּדְּבָרִ֔ים אֲשֶׁ֥ר הוֹדִ֖יעוּ לָהֶֽם׃ ס ¹³וּבַיּ֣וֹם הַשֵּׁנִ֡י נֶאֶסְפוּ֩ רָאשֵׁ֨י הָאָב֜וֹת לְכָל־הָעָ֗ם הַכֹּהֲנִ֣ים וְהַלְוִיִּ֔ם אֶל־עֶזְרָ֖א הַסֹּפֵ֑ר וּֽלְהַשְׂכִּ֖יל אֶל־דִּבְרֵ֥י הַתּוֹרָֽה׃ ¹⁴וַֽיִּמְצְא֖וּ כָּת֣וּב בַּתּוֹרָ֑ה אֲשֶׁ֨ר צִוָּ֤ה יְהוָה֙ בְּיַד־מֹשֶׁ֔ה אֲשֶׁר֩ יֵשְׁב֨וּ בְנֵֽי־יִשְׂרָאֵ֧ל בַּסֻּכּ֛וֹת בֶּחָ֖ג בַּחֹ֥דֶשׁ הַשְּׁבִיעִֽי׃ ¹⁵וַאֲשֶׁ֣ר יַשְׁמִ֗יעוּ וְיַעֲבִ֨ירוּ ק֥וֹל בְּכָל־עָרֵיהֶם֮ וּבִירוּשָׁלַ֣͏ִם לֵאמֹר֒ צְא֣וּ הָהָ֗ר וְהָבִ֨יאוּ֙ עֲלֵי־זַ֔יִת וַעֲלֵי־עֵ֣ץ שֶׁ֔מֶן וַעֲלֵ֤י הֲדַס֙ וַעֲלֵ֣י תְמָרִ֔ים וַעֲלֵ֖י עֵ֣ץ עָבֹ֑ת לַעֲשֹׂ֥ת סֻכֹּ֖ת כַּכָּתֽוּב׃ פ ¹⁶וַיֵּצְא֣וּ הָעָם֮ וַיָּבִיאוּ֒ וַיַּעֲשׂ֨וּ לָהֶ֤ם סֻכּוֹת֙ אִ֣ישׁ עַל־גַּגּ֔וֹ וּבְחַצְרֹ֣תֵיהֶ֔ם וּבְחַצְר֖וֹת בֵּ֣ית הָאֱלֹהִ֑ים וּבִרְחוֹב֙ שַׁ֣עַר הַמַּ֔יִם וּבִרְח֖וֹב ¹⁷שַׁ֥עַר אֶפְרָֽיִם׃ וַֽיַּעֲשׂ֣וּ כָל־הַ֠קָּהָל

hills, and bring olive branches and [2]wild olive branches, myrtle branches, palm branches and branches of *other* leafy trees, to make booths, as it is written." **16** So the people went out and brought *them* and made booths for themselves, each [a]on his roof, and in their courts and in the courts of the house of God, and in the square at [b]the Water Gate and in the square at [c]the Gate of Ephraim. **17** The entire assembly of those who had returned from the captivity made booths and lived in [1]them. The sons of Israel [a]had indeed not done so from the days of Joshua the son of Nun to that day. And [b]there was great rejoicing. **18** [a]He read from the book of the law of God daily, from the first day to the last day. And they [b]celebrated the feast seven days, and on [c]the eighth day *there was* a solemn assembly according to the ordinance.

הַשָּׁבִים מִן־הַשְּׁבִי ׀ סֻכּוֹת וַיֵּשְׁבוּ בַסֻּכּוֹת כִּי לֹא־עָשׂוּ מִימֵי יֵשׁוּעַ בִּן־נוּן כֵּן בְּנֵי יִשְׂרָאֵל עַד הַיּוֹם הַהוּא וַתְּהִי שִׂמְחָה גְּדוֹלָה מְאֹד׃ **18** וַיִּקְרָא בְּסֵפֶר תּוֹרַת הָאֱלֹהִים יוֹם ׀ בְּיוֹם מִן־הַיּוֹם הָרִאשׁוֹן עַד הַיּוֹם הָאַחֲרוֹן וַיַּעֲשׂוּ־חָג שִׁבְעַת יָמִים וּבַיּוֹם הַשְּׁמִינִי עֲצֶרֶת כַּמִּשְׁפָּט׃ פ

References

Nehemiah 8:1
[1]Lit *said to*
[2]Lit *commanded*
[a]Neh 3:26
[b]Ezra 7:6
[c]2 Chr 34:15

Nehemiah 8:2
[a]Deut 31:9-11; Neh 8:9
[b]Lev 23:24

Nehemiah 8:3
[1]Lit *the light*
[a]Neh 8:1

Nehemiah 8:5
[a]Neh 8:3
[b]Judg 3:20; 1 Kin 8:12-14

Nehemiah 8:6
[a]Neh 5:13
[b]Ex 4:31

Nehemiah 8:8
[1]Or *explaining*

Nehemiah 8:9
[1]Heb *Tirshatha,* a Persian title
[a]Neh 7:65, 70
[b]Neh 12:26
[c]Neh 8:2
[d]Deut 12:7, 12

Nehemiah 8:10
[a]Deut 26:11-13

Nehemiah 8:12
[1]Lit *make a great rejoicing*
[a]Neh 8:10
[b]Neh 8:7, 8

Nehemiah 8:14
[a]Lev 23:34, 40, 42

Nehemiah 8:15
[1]Lit *And that they will cause to be heard*
[2]Lit *oil tree,* species unknown
[a]Lev 23:4
[b]Deut 16:16
[c]Lev 23:40

Nehemiah 8:16
[a]Jer 32:29
[b]Neh 8:1
[c]2 Kin 14:13; Neh 12:39

Nehemiah 8:17
[1]Lit *the booths*
[a]2 Chr 7:8; 8:13
[b]2 Chr 30:21

Nehemiah 8:18
[a]Deut 31:11
[b]Lev 23:36
[c]Num 29:35

Process of Discovery

  Linguistics Section

  Linguistic Structure

[The Gathering] [1] And all the people gathered as one man at the square which was in front of *a*the Water Gate, and they [1]asked *b*Ezra the scribe to bring *c*the book of the law of Moses which the LORD had [2]given to Israel.

[Reading the Torah] [2] Then *a*Ezra the priest brought the law before the assembly of men, women and all who *could* listen with understanding, on *b*the first day of the seventh month. [3] He read from it before the square which was in front of *a*the Water Gate from [1]early morning until midday, in the presence of men and women, those who could understand; and all the people were attentive to the book of the law. [4] Ezra the scribe stood at a wooden podium which they had made for the purpose. And beside him stood Mattithiah, Shema, Anaiah, Uriah, Hilkiah, and Maaseiah on his right hand; and Pedaiah, Mishael, Malchijah, Hashum, Hashbaddanah, Zechariah *and* Meshullam on his left hand. [5] Ezra opened *a*the book in the sight of all the people for he was standing above all the people; and when he opened it, all the people *b*stood up. [6] Then Ezra blessed the LORD the great God. And all the people answered, "*a*Amen, Amen!" while lifting up their hands; then *b*they bowed low and worshiped the LORD with *their* faces to the ground. [7] Also Jeshua, Bani, Sherebiah, Jamin, Akkub, Shabbethai, Hodiah, Maaseiah, Kelita, Azariah, Jozabad, Hanan, Pelaiah, the Levites, explained the law to the people while the people *remained* in their place. [8] They read from the book, from the law of God, [1]translating to give the sense so that they understood the reading.

[Declaration of a holy day] [9] Then Nehemiah, who was the [1]*a*governor, and Ezra *b*the priest *and* scribe, and the Levites who taught the people said to all the people, "*c*This day is holy to the LORD your God; *d*do not mourn or weep." For all the people were weeping when they heard the words of the law. [10] Then he said to them, "Go, eat of the fat, drink of the sweet, and *a*send portions to him who has nothing prepared; for this day is holy to our Lord. Do not be grieved, for the joy of the LORD is your strength." [11] So the Levites calmed all the people, saying, "Be still, for the day is holy; do not be grieved." [12] All the people went away to eat, to drink, *a*to send portions and to [1]celebrate a great festival, *b*because they understood the words which had been made known to them.

[More commandments] [13] Then on the second day the heads of fathers' *households* of all the people, the priests and the Levites were gathered to Ezra the scribe that they might gain insight into the words of the law. [14] They found written in the law how the LORD had commanded through Moses that the sons of Israel *a*should live in booths during the feast of the seventh month. [15] [1a]So they proclaimed and circulated a proclamation in all their cities and *b*in Jerusalem, saying, "[c]Go out to the hills, and bring olive branches and [2]wild olive branches, myrtle branches, palm branches and branches of *other* leafy trees, to make booths, as it is written." [16] So the people went out and brought *them* and made booths for themselves, each *a*on his roof, and in their courts and in the courts of the house of God, and in the square at *b*the Water Gate and in the square at *c*the Gate of Ephraim. [17] The entire assembly of those who had returned from the captivity made booths and lived in [1]them. The sons of Israel *a*had indeed not done so from the days of Joshua the son of Nun to that day. And *b*there was great rejoicing. [18] *a*He read from the book of the law of God daily, from the first day to the last day. And they *b*celebrated the feast seven days, and on *c*the eighth day *there was* a solemn assembly according to the ordinance.

Discussion

This chapter describes the reading of the Torah to the people and their acceptance of it.

Questioning the Passage

1. Why was the Torah called the "book of Moses?"

    Moses had received the Law from the LORD in the form of two tablets, the Ten commandments. When he came down the mountain, he discovered that Israel was engaging in idolatry and other passion crimes. Moses became so angry with the people that he threw the two tablets, created by the finger of the LORD, onto the ground. This action shattered the tablets. Moses then returned to the LORD and asked for a second set of tablets. This time the LORD told Moses that he needed to write down what the LORD said. Thus, the second set of tablets is called the Law of Moses because Moses carved these tablets.

2. What is the significance of the first day of the seventh month? (v. 2)

    The seventh month is Tishrei. The first day of Tishrei is Rosh Hashannah.[iv34]

3. What I s succot? (v. 18)

    Verse eighteen describes the Succot celebration. During the Exile, the ritualistic working of Succot was not celebrated. Now that Nehemiah was the government of Judah, he reinstituted the celebration.

Biblical Personalities

1. Ezra was the primary Scribe who had returned to Jerusalem when the Exile to Babylon was over.

2. Mattithiah, Shema, Anaiah, Uriah, Hilkiah, and Maaseiah on his right hand; and Pedaiah, Mishael, Malchijah, Hashum, Hashbaddanah, Zechariah *and* Meshullam on his left hand. These were the men who stood with Ezra when he read from the Torah.

3. Jeshua, Bani, Sherebiah, Jamin, Akkub, Shabbethai, Hodiah, Maaseiah, Kelita, Azariah, Jozabad, Hanan, Pelaiah, the Levites were the teachers who explained the law to the people while the people *remained* in their place.

4. The following men stood on the right or left of Ezra when he read the Torah to the people. Mattithiah, Shema, Anaiah, Uriah, Hilkiah, and Maaseiah on

---

[34] Nosson Scherman and Meir Zlotowitz, *The Writings = Kesuvim / The Writings: with a Commentary Anthologized from Rabbinic Writings = Ketuvim: 'im Perush Rashi, Metsudat Dayid, Metsudat Tsiyon, ye-'od* (Brooklyn, NY: Mesorah Publications, 2016).

his right hand; and Pedaiah, Mishael, Malchijah, Hashum, Hashbaddanah, Zechariah *and* Meshullam on his left hand.

Phrase Study

1. תִּרְשָׁתָא *(tirshātāʾ) Tirshatha.* (ASV and RSV "governor.") (v. 9)

"The word is attested five times in the OT (only in Ezr and Neh) and is always preceded by the definite article. It is a noun of Persian derivation meaning approximately "(His) Excellency, (His) Honor." A comparison of Neh 8:9 with 12:26 demonstrates that it is the Persian functional equivalent of פֶּחָה "governor," a noun of Akkadian derivation that appears in the latter verse. Nehemiah himself is the תִּרְשָׁתָא in 8:9 and 10:1 [H 2]; an unnamed individual bears the title [Vol. 2, p. 982] in Ezr 2:63 and Neh 7:65, 69. If the latter was a native Persian, it is noteworthy that he nevertheless concerned himself with religious as well as political matters among a people some of whom were unable to prove their Israelite ancestry. Nehemiah's own role as governor likewise did not prevent him from taking an active part in the spiritual life of his people. To this day, he serves as a parade example of a dedicated political leader who, though bearing an alien title, acted uncompromisingly whenever and wherever spiritual issues were at stake."[35]

---

[35] R. Laird Harris, Gleason L. Archer, and Bruce K. Waltke, *Theological Wordbook of the Old Testament* (Chicago: Moody Press, 2004).

Thoughts

Nehemiah was a wise and faithful governor of Judea. He reinstated the traditions of the people and the worship to the LORD. Nehemiah stood for the restoration of the ways of the Torah. By reestablishing Succot and reading from the Torah, Nehemiah showed the people how important it was to follow the LORD's Word.

Chapter Nine

Language

New American Standard 1995	Hebrew
Neh. 9:1 Now on the twenty-fourth day of [a]this month the sons of Israel assembled [b]with fasting, in sackcloth and with [c]dirt upon them. [2] The [1a]descendants of Israel separated themselves from all foreigners, and stood and [b]confessed their sins and the iniquities of their fathers. [3] While [a]they stood in their place, they read from the book of the law of the LORD their God for a fourth of the day; and for *another* fourth they confessed and worshiped the LORD their God. [4] [a]Now on the Levites' platform stood Jeshua, Bani, Kadmiel, Shebaniah, Bunni, Sherebiah, Bani *and* Chenani, and they cried with a loud voice to the LORD their God.	א וּבְיוֹם֩ עֶשְׂרִ֨ים וְאַרְבָּעָ֜ה לַחֹ֣דֶשׁ הַזֶּ֗ה נֶאֶסְפ֤וּ בְנֵֽי־יִשְׂרָאֵל֙ בְּצ֔וֹם וּבְשַׂקִּ֖ים וַאֲדָמָ֥ה עֲלֵיהֶֽם׃ ²וַיִּבָּֽדְלוּ֙ זֶ֣רַע יִשְׂרָאֵ֔ל מִכֹּ֖ל בְּנֵ֣י נֵכָ֑ר וַיַּעַמְד֗וּ וַיִּתְוַדּוּ֙ עַל־חַטֹּ֣אתֵיהֶ֔ם וַעֲוֺנ֖וֹת אֲבֹתֵיהֶֽם׃ ³וַיָּק֙וּמוּ֙ עַל־עָמְדָ֔ם וַֽיִּקְרְא֗וּ בְּסֵ֛פֶר תּוֹרַ֛ת יְהוָ֥ה אֱלֹהֵיהֶ֖ם רְבִעִ֣ית הַיּ֑וֹם וּרְבִעִית֙ מִתְוַדִּ֣ים וּמִֽשְׁתַּחֲוִ֔ים לַיהוָ֖ה אֱלֹהֵיהֶֽם׃ פ ⁴וַיָּ֜קָם עַֽל־מַעֲלֵ֣ה הַלְוִיִּ֗ם יֵשׁ֨וּעַ וּבָנִ֜י קַדְמִיאֵ֧ל שְׁבַנְיָ֛ה בֻּנִּ֥י שֵׁרֵבְיָ֖ה בָּנִ֣י כְנָ֑נִי וַֽיִּזְעֲקוּ֙ בְּק֣וֹל גָּד֔וֹל אֶל־יְהוָ֖ה אֱלֹהֵיהֶֽם׃
Neh. 9:5 Then the Levites, Jeshua, Kadmiel, Bani, Hashabneiah, Sherebiah, Hodiah, Shebaniah *and* Pethahiah, said, "Arise, bless the LORD your God forever and ever!	⁵וַיֹּאמְר֣וּ הַלְוִיִּ֡ם יֵשׁ֣וּעַ וְ֠קַדְמִיאֵל בָּנִ֨י חֲשַׁבְנְיָ֜ה שֵׁרֵֽבְיָ֤ה הֽוֹדִיָּה֙ שְׁבַנְיָ֣ה פְתַֽחְיָ֔ה ק֗וּמוּ בָּרֲכוּ֙ אֶת־יְהוָ֣ה
O may Your glorious name be blessed	אֱלֹֽהֵיכֶ֔ם מִן־הָעוֹלָ֖ם עַד־הָעוֹלָ֑ם
And exalted above all blessing and praise!	וִיבָֽרְכוּ֙ שֵׁ֣ם כְּבוֹדֶ֔ךָ
[6] "[a]You alone are the LORD.	וּמְרוֹמַ֥ם עַל־כָּל־בְּרָכָ֖ה
[b]You have made the heavens, The heaven of heavens with all their host, The earth and all that is on it, The seas and all that is in them. [c]You give life to all of them	⁶אַתָּה־ה֣וּא יְהוָה֮ וְתֶהַלָּֽה׃

And the heavenly host bows down before You.

7   "You are the LORD God,
    *Who chose Abram
    And brought him out from *Ur of the Chaldees,
    And *gave him the name Abraham.

8   "You found *his heart faithful before You,
    And made a covenant with him
    To give *him* the land of the Canaanite,
    Of the Hittite and the Amorite,
    Of the Perizzite, the Jebusite and the Girgashite —
    To give *it* to his ¹descendants.
    And You *have fulfilled Your promise,
    For You are righteous.

Neh. 9:9   "*You saw the affliction of our fathers in Egypt,
    And *heard their cry by the ¹Red Sea.

10   "Then You performed *signs and wonders against Pharaoh,
    Against all his servants and all the people of his land;
    For You knew that *they acted arrogantly toward them,
    And *made a name for Yourself as *it is* this day.

11   "*You divided the sea before them,
    So they passed through the midst of the sea on dry ground;
    And *their pursuers You hurled into the depths,
    Like a stone into ¹raging waters.

12   "And with a pillar of cloud *You led them by day,
    And with a pillar of fire by night

לְבַדֶּךָ אַתְּ [אַתָּה] עָשִׂיתָ אֶת־
הַשָּׁמַיִם שְׁמֵי הַשָּׁמַיִם וְכָל־
צְבָאָם הָאָרֶץ וְכָל־אֲשֶׁר עָלֶיהָ
הַיַּמִּים וְכָל־אֲשֶׁר בָּהֶם וְאַתָּה
מְחַיֶּה אֶת־כֻּלָּם וּצְבָא הַשָּׁמַיִם
אַתָּה־הוּא ⁷לְךָ מִשְׁתַּחֲוִים׃
יְהוָה הָאֱלֹהִים אֲשֶׁר בָּחַרְתָּ
בְּאַבְרָם וְהוֹצֵאתוֹ מֵאוּר
כַּשְׂדִּים וְשַׂמְתָּ שְּׁמוֹ אַבְרָהָם׃ ⁸
וּמָצָאתָ אֶת־לְבָבוֹ נֶאֱמָן לְפָנֶיךָ
וְכָרוֹת עִמּוֹ הַבְּרִית לָתֵת אֶת־
אֶרֶץ הַכְּנַעֲנִי הַחִתִּי הָאֱמֹרִי
וְהַפְּרִזִּי וְהַיְבוּסִי וְהַגִּרְגָּשִׁי
לָתֵת לְזַרְעוֹ וַתָּקֶם אֶת־דְּבָרֶיךָ
וַתֵּרֶא אֶת־ ⁹כִּי צַדִּיק אָתָּה׃
עֳנִי אֲבֹתֵינוּ בְּמִצְרָיִם וְאֶת־
זַעֲקָתָם שָׁמַעְתָּ עַל־יַם־סוּף׃ ¹⁰
וַתִּתֵּן אֹתֹת וּמֹפְתִים בְּפַרְעֹה
וּבְכָל־עֲבָדָיו וּבְכָל־עַם אַרְצוֹ
כִּי יָדַעְתָּ כִּי הֵזִידוּ עֲלֵיהֶם
וַתַּעַשׂ־לְךָ שֵׁם כְּהַיּוֹם הַזֶּה׃
וְהַיָּם בָּקַעְתָּ לִפְנֵיהֶם ¹¹
וַיַּעַבְרוּ בְתוֹךְ־הַיָּם בַּיַּבָּשָׁה
וְאֶת־רֹדְפֵיהֶם הִשְׁלַכְתָּ
בִמְצוֹלֹת כְּמוֹ־אֶבֶן בְּמַיִם

To light for them the way
In which they were to go.

13 "Then *a*You came down on Mount Sinai,

And *b*spoke with them from heaven;

You gave them *c*just ordinances and true laws,

Good statutes and commandments.

14 "So You made known to them *a*Your holy sabbath,

And laid down for them commandments, statutes and law,

Through Your servant Moses.

15 "You *a*provided bread from heaven for them for their hunger,

You *b*brought forth water from a rock for them for their thirst,

And You *c*told them to enter in order to possess

The land which You [1]swore to give them.

Neh. 9:16 "But they, our fathers, *a*acted arrogantly;

They [1b]became stubborn and would not listen to Your commandments.

17 "They refused to listen,

And *a*did not remember Your wondrous deeds which You had performed among them;

So they became stubborn and *b*appointed a leader to return to their slavery [1]in Egypt.

But You are a God *c*of forgiveness,

Gracious and compassionate,

Slow to anger and abounding in lovingkindness;

And You did not forsake them.

וּבְעַמּוּד עָנָן ‬12‬ עַזַּיִם ׃

הִנְחִיתָם יוֹמָם וּבְעַמּוּד אֵשׁ

לַיְלָה לְהָאִיר לָהֶם אֶת־הַדֶּרֶךְ

וְעַל הַר־‬13‬ אֲשֶׁר יֵלְכוּ־בָהּ ׃

סִינַי יָרַדְתָּ וְדַבֵּר עִמָּהֶם

מִשָּׁמַיִם וַתִּתֵּן לָהֶם מִשְׁפָּטִים

יְשָׁרִים וְתוֹרוֹת אֱמֶת חֻקִּים

וְאֶת־שַׁבַּת ‬14‬ וּמִצְוֺת טוֹבִים ׃

קָדְשְׁךָ הוֹדַעַתָ לָהֶם וּמִצְוֺת

וְחֻקִּים וְתוֹרָה צִוִּיתָ לָהֶם בְּיַד

וְלֶחֶם מִשָּׁמַיִם ‬15‬ מֹשֶׁה עַבְדֶּךָ ׃

נָתַתָּה לָהֶם לִרְעָבָם וּמַיִם

מִסֶּלַע הוֹצֵאתָ לָהֶם לִצְמָאָם

וַתֹּאמֶר לָהֶם לָבוֹא לָרֶשֶׁת אֶת־

הָאָרֶץ אֲשֶׁר־נָשָׂאתָ אֶת־יָדְךָ

וְהֵם וַאֲבֹתֵינוּ ‬16‬ לָתֵת לָהֶם ׃

הֵזִידוּ וַיַּקְשׁוּ אֶת־עָרְפָּם וְלֹא

וַיְמָאֲנוּ ‬17‬ שָׁמְעוּ אֶל־מִצְוֺתֶיךָ ׃

לִשְׁמֹעַ וְלֹא־זָכְרוּ נִפְלְאֹתֶיךָ

אֲשֶׁר עָשִׂיתָ עִמָּהֶם וַיַּקְשׁוּ אֶת־

עָרְפָּם וַיִּתְּנוּ־רֹאשׁ לָשׁוּב

לְעַבְדֻתָם בְּמִרְיָם וְאַתָּה אֱלוֹהַּ

סְלִיחוֹת חַנּוּן וְרַחוּם אֶרֶךְ־

אַפַּיִם וְרַב־וְחֶסֶד [חֶסֶד] וְלֹא

אַף כִּי־עָשׂוּ לָהֶם ‬18‬ עֲזַבְתָּם ׃

18 "Even when they ᵃmade for themselves

A calf of molten metal

And said, 'This is your God

Who brought you up from Egypt,'

And committed great ¹blasphemies,

19 ᵃYou, in Your great compassion,

Did not forsake them in the wilderness;

ᵇThe pillar of cloud did not leave them by day,

To guide them on their way,

Nor the pillar of fire by night, to light for them the way in which they were to go.

20 "ᵃYou gave Your good Spirit to instruct them,

Your manna You did not withhold from their mouth,

And You gave them water for their thirst.

21 "Indeed, ᵃforty years You provided for them in the wilderness *and* they were not in want;

Their clothes did not wear out, nor did their feet swell.

22 "You also gave them kingdoms and peoples,

And allotted *them* to them as a ¹boundary.

ᵃThey took possession of the land of Sihon ²the king of Heshbon

And the land of Og the king of Bashan.

23 "You made their sons numerous as ᵃthe stars of heaven,

And You brought them into the land

Which You had told their fathers to enter and possess.

עֵ֣גֶל מַסֵּכָ֗ה וַיֹּ֣אמְר֔וּ זֶ֣ה אֱלֹהֶ֔יךָ

אֲשֶׁ֥ר הֶעֶלְךָ֖ מִמִּצְרָ֑יִם וַֽיַּעֲשׂ֔וּ

וְאַתָּה֙ 19 נֶֽאָצ֖וֹת גְּדֹלֽוֹת:

בְּרַחֲמֶ֣יךָ הָֽרַבִּ֗ים לֹ֤א עֲזַבְתָּם֙

בַּמִּדְבָּ֔ר אֶת־עַמּ֣וּד הֶֽעָנָ֡ן לֹא־

סָ֣ר מֵֽעֲלֵיהֶ֣ם בְּיוֹמָ֗ם לְהַנְחֹתָ֤ם

בְּהַדֶּ֨רֶךְ֙ וְאֶת־עַמּ֤וּד הָאֵשׁ֙

בְּלַ֔יְלָה לְהָאִ֣יר לָהֶ֔ם וְאֶת־

20 הַדֶּ֖רֶךְ אֲשֶׁ֥ר יֵֽלְכוּ־בָֽהּ:

וְרֽוּחֲךָ֣ הַטּוֹבָ֗ה נָתַ֖תָּ לְהַשְׂכִּילָ֑ם

וּמַנְךָ֙ לֹא־מָנַ֣עְתָּ מִפִּיהֶ֔ם וּמַ֛יִם

21 נָתַ֥תָּה לָהֶ֖ם לִצְמָאָֽם:

וְאַרְבָּעִ֥ים שָׁנָ֛ה כִּלְכַּלְתָּ֥ם

בַּמִּדְבָּ֖ר לֹ֣א חָסֵ֑רוּ שַׂלְמֹֽתֵיהֶם֙

לֹ֣א בָל֔וּ וְרַגְלֵיהֶ֖ם לֹ֥א בָצֵֽקוּ:

22 וַתִּתֵּ֨ן לָהֶ֤ם מַמְלָכוֹת֙

וַֽעֲמָמִ֔ים וַתַּחְלְקֵ֖ם לְפֵאָ֑ה

וַיִּֽירְשׁ֞וּ אֶת־אֶ֣רֶץ סִיח֗וֹן וְאֶת־

אֶ֨רֶץ֙ מֶ֣לֶךְ חֶשְׁבּ֔וֹן וְאֶת־אֶ֖רֶץ

23 ע֖וֹג מֶֽלֶךְ־הַבָּשָֽׁן: וּבְנֵיהֶ֣ם

הִרְבִּ֔יתָ כְּכֹכְבֵ֖י הַשָּׁמָ֑יִם

וַתְּבִיאֵם֙ אֶל־הָאָ֔רֶץ אֲשֶׁר־

אָמַ֥רְתָּ לַֽאֲבֹתֵיהֶ֖ם לָב֣וֹא

24 לָרָֽשֶׁת: וַיָּבֹ֤אוּ הַבָּנִים֙

וַיִּֽירְשׁ֣וּ אֶת־הָאָ֔רֶץ וַתַּכְנַ֨ע

100

24 "*a*So their sons entered and possessed the land.

And *b*You subdued before them the inhabitants of the land, the Canaanites,

And You gave them into their hand, with their kings and the peoples of the land,

To do with them [1]as they desired.

25 "*a*They captured fortified cities and a [1]*b*fertile land.

They took possession of *c*houses full of every good thing,

Hewn cisterns, vineyards, olive groves,

Fruit trees in abundance.

So they ate, were filled and *d*grew fat,

And *e*reveled in Your great goodness.

Neh. 9:26 "*a*But they became disobedient and rebelled against You,

And *b*cast Your law behind their backs

And *c*killed Your prophets who had *d*admonished them

So that they might return to You,

And *e*they committed great [1]blasphemies.

27 "Therefore You *a*delivered them into the hand of their oppressors who oppressed them,

But when they cried to You *b*in the time of their distress,

You heard from heaven, and according to Your great compassion

You *c*gave them deliverers who delivered them from the hand of their oppressors.

לִפְנֵיהֶם אֶת־יֹשְׁבֵי הָאָרֶץ הַכְּנַעֲנִים וַתִּתְּנֵם בְּיָדָם וְאֶת־ מַלְכֵיהֶם וְאֶת־עַמְמֵי הָאָרֶץ ²⁵ לַעֲשׂוֹת בָּהֶם כִּרְצוֹנָם׃

וַיִּלְכְּדוּ עָרִים בְּצֻרוֹת וַאֲדָמָה שְׁמֵנָה וַיִּירְשׁוּ בָּתִּים מְלֵאִים־ כָּל־טוּב בֹּרוֹת חֲצוּבִים כְּרָמִים וְזֵיתִים וְעֵץ מַאֲכָל לָרֹב וַיֹּאכְלוּ וַיִּשְׂבְּעוּ וַיַּשְׁמִינוּ ²⁶ וַיִּתְעַדְּנוּ בְּטוּבְךָ הַגָּדוֹל׃

וַיַּמְרוּ וַיִּמְרְדוּ בָּךְ וַיַּשְׁלִכוּ אֶת־ תּוֹרָתְךָ אַחֲרֵי גַוָּם וְאֶת־נְבִיאֶיךָ הָרָגוּ אֲשֶׁר־הֵעִידוּ בָם לַהֲשִׁיבָם אֵלֶיךָ וַיַּעֲשׂוּ נֶאָצוֹת גְּדוֹלֹת׃ ²⁷ וַתִּתְּנֵם בְּיַד צָרֵיהֶם וַיָּצֵרוּ לָהֶם וּבְעֵת צָרָתָם יִצְעֲקוּ אֵלֶיךָ וְאַתָּה מִשָּׁמַיִם תִּשְׁמָע וּכְרַחֲמֶיךָ הָרַבִּים תִּתֵּן לָהֶם מוֹשִׁיעִים ²⁸ וְיוֹשִׁיעוּם מִיַּד צָרֵיהֶם׃ וּכְנוֹחַ לָהֶם יָשׁוּבוּ לַעֲשׂוֹת רַע לְפָנֶיךָ וַתַּעַזְבֵם בְּיַד אֹיְבֵיהֶם וַיִּרְדּוּ בָהֶם וַיָּשׁוּבוּ וַיִּזְעָקוּךָ וְאַתָּה מִשָּׁמַיִם תִּשְׁמַע וְתַצִּילֵם ²⁹ כְּרַחֲמֶיךָ רַבּוֹת עִתִּים וַתָּעַד בָּהֶם לַהֲשִׁיבָם אֶל־

28 "But [a]as soon as they had rest, they did evil again before You;

Therefore You abandoned them to the hand of their enemies, so that they ruled over them.

When they cried again to You, You heard from heaven,

And [b]many times You rescued them according to Your compassion,

29 And [a]admonished them in order to turn them back to Your law.

Yet [b]they acted arrogantly and did not listen to Your commandments but sinned against Your ordinances,

By [c]which if a man observes them he shall live.

And they [1d]turned a stubborn shoulder and stiffened their neck, and would not listen.

30 "[a]However, You bore with them for many years,

And [b]admonished them by [c]Your Spirit through Your prophets,

Yet they would not give ear.

Therefore You gave them into the hand of the peoples of the lands.

31 "Nevertheless, in Your great compassion You [a]did not make an end of them or forsake them,

For You are [b]a gracious and compassionate God.

Neh. 9:32 "Now therefore, our God, [a]the great, the mighty, and the awesome God, who keeps covenant and lovingkindness,

Do not let all the hardship seem insignificant before You,

Which has come upon us, our kings, our princes, our priests, our

תּוֹרָתֶ֔ךָ וְהֵ֥מָּה הֵזִ֖ידוּ וְלֹא־
שָׁמְע֣וּ לְמִצְוֺתֶ֗יךָ וּבְמִשְׁפָּטֶ֛יךָ
חָֽטְאוּ־בָ֔ם אֲשֶׁר־יַעֲשֶׂ֥ה אָדָ֖ם
וְחָיָ֣ה בָהֶ֑ם וַיִּתְּנ֤וּ כָתֵף֙ סוֹרֶ֔רֶת
30 וְעָרְפָּ֥ם הִקְשׁ֖וּ וְלֹ֥א שָׁמֵֽעוּ׃
וַתִּמְשֹׁ֤ךְ עֲלֵיהֶם֙ שָׁנִ֣ים רַבּ֔וֹת
וַתָּ֨עַד בָּ֧ם בְּרוּחֲךָ֛ בְּיַד־נְבִיאֶ֖יךָ
וְלֹ֣א הֶאֱזִ֑ינוּ וַֽתִּתְּנֵ֔ם בְּיַ֖ד עַמֵּ֥י
31 הָאֲרָצֹ֑ת וּֽבְרַחֲמֶ֣יךָ הָרַבִּ֗ים
לֹֽא־עֲשִׂיתָ֥ם כָּלָ֖ה וְלֹ֣א עֲזַבְתָּ֑ם
32 כִּ֛י אֵ֥ל חַנּ֥וּן וְרַח֖וּם אָֽתָּה׃
וְעַתָּ֣ה אֱלֹהֵ֡ינוּ הָאֵל֩ הַגָּד֨וֹל
הַגִּבּ֜וֹר וְהַנּוֹרָא֮ שׁוֹמֵ֣ר הַבְּרִ֣ית
וְהַחֶ֒סֶד֒ אַל־יִמְעַ֣ט לְפָנֶ֡יךָ אֵ֣ת
כָּל־הַתְּלָאָ֣ה אֲֽשֶׁר־מְ֠צָאַתְנוּ
לִמְלָכֵ֨ינוּ לְשָׂרֵ֜ינוּ וּלְכֹהֲנֵ֗ינוּ
וְלִנְבִיאֵ֙נוּ֙ וְלַאֲבֹתֵ֔ינוּ וּלְכָל־
עַמֶּ֑ךָ מִימֵי֙ מַלְכֵ֣י אַשּׁ֔וּר עַ֖ד
33 הַיּ֥וֹם הַזֶּֽה׃ וְאַתָּ֣ה צַדִּ֔יק
עַ֖ל כָּל־הַבָּ֣א עָלֵ֑ינוּ כִּֽי־אֱמֶ֥ת
34 עָשִׂ֖יתָ וַאֲנַ֥חְנוּ הִרְשָֽׁעְנוּ׃
וְאֶת־מְלָכֵ֨ינוּ שָׂרֵ֜ינוּ כֹּהֲנֵ֗ינוּ
וַאֲבֹתֵ֗ינוּ לֹ֤א עָשׂוּ֙ תּוֹרָתֶ֔ךָ וְלֹ֣א
הִקְשִׁ֣יבוּ אֶל־מִצְוֺתֶ֔יךָ
וּלְעֵדְוֺתֶ֕יךָ אֲשֶׁ֖ר הַעִידֹ֥תָ בָּהֶֽם׃

prophets, our fathers and on all Your people,

[b]From the days of the kings of Assyria to this day.

33 "However, [a]You are just in all that has come upon us;

For You have dealt faithfully, but we have acted wickedly.

34 "For our kings, our leaders, our priests and our fathers have not kept Your law

Or paid attention to Your commandments and Your [1]admonitions with which You have [2]admonished them.

35 "But [a]they, in their own kingdom,

[b]With Your great goodness which You gave them,

With the broad and rich land which You set before them,

Did not serve You or turn from their evil deeds.

36 "Behold, [a]we are slaves today,

And as to the land which You gave to our fathers to eat of its fruit and its bounty,

Behold, we are slaves in it.

37 "[a]Its abundant produce is for the kings

Whom You have set over us because of our sins;

They also rule over our bodies

And over our cattle as they please,

So we are in great distress.

Neh. 9:38 "[1]Now because of all this

[a]We are making an agreement in writing;

And on the [b]sealed document *are the names of* our leaders, our Levites *and* our priests."

וְהֵם בְּמַלְכוּתָם וּבְטוּבְךָ 35 הָרָב אֲשֶׁר־נָתַתָּ לָהֶם וּבָאָרֶץ הָרְחָבָה וְהַשְּׁמֵנָה אֲשֶׁר־נָתַתָּ לִפְנֵיהֶם לֹא עֲבָדוּךָ וְלֹא־שָׁבוּ 36 מִמַּעַלְלֵיהֶם הָרָעִים: הִנֵּה אֲנַחְנוּ הַיּוֹם עֲבָדִים וְהָאָרֶץ אֲשֶׁר־נָתַתָּה לַאֲבֹתֵינוּ לֶאֱכֹל אֶת־פִּרְיָהּ וְאֶת־טוּבָהּ הִנֵּה 37 אֲנַחְנוּ עֲבָדִים עָלֶיהָ: וּתְבוּאָתָהּ מַרְבָּה לַמְּלָכִים אֲשֶׁר־נָתַתָּה עָלֵינוּ בְּחַטֹּאותֵינוּ וְעַל גְּוִיֹּתֵינוּ מֹשְׁלִים וּבִבְהֶמְתֵּנוּ כִּרְצוֹנָם וּבְצָרָה גְדוֹלָה אֲנַחְנוּ:
פ

References

Nehemiah 9:1
[a]Neh 8:2
[b]Ezra 8:23
[c]1 Sam 4:12

Nehemiah 9:2
[1]Lit *seed*
[a]Ezra 10:11; Neh 13:3
[b]Prov 28:13; Jer 3:13

Nehemiah 9:3
[a]Neh 8:4

Nehemiah 9:4
[a]Neh 8:7

Nehemiah 9:6
[a]Deut 6:4; 2 Kin 19:15
[b]Gen 1:1
[c]Col 1:16f

Nehemiah 9:7
[a]Gen 12:1
[b]Gen 11:31
[c]Gen 17:5

Nehemiah 9:8
[1]Lit *seed*
[a]Gen 15:6, 18-21
[b]Josh 21:43-45

Nehemiah 9:9
[1]Lit *Sea of Reeds*
[a]Ex 3:7
[b]Ex 14:10-14, 31

Nehemiah 9:10
[a]Ex 7:8-12:32
[b]Ex 5:2

Nehemiah 9:19
[a]Deut 8:2-4; Neh 9:27, 31
[b]Neh 9:12

Nehemiah 9:20
[a]Num 11:17; Neh 9:30; Is 63:11-14

Nehemiah 9:21
[a]Deut 2:7

Nehemiah 9:22
[1]Lit *side, corner*
[2]So the Gr and the Latin; Heb reads *and the land of the king of Heshbon*
[a]Num 21:21-35

Nehemiah 9:23
[a]Gen 15:5; 22:17

Nehemiah 9:24
[1]Lit *according to their desire*
[a]Josh 11:23; 21:43
[b]Josh 18:1

Nehemiah 9:25
[1]Lit *fat*
[a]Deut 3:5
[b]Num 13:27
[c]Deut 6:11
[d]Deut 32:15
[e]1 Kin 8:66

Nehemiah 9:26
[1]Lit *acts of contempt*
[a]Judg 2:11
[b]1 Kin 14:9
[c]2 Chr 36:16
[d]Neh 9:30
[e]Neh 9:18

[c]Ex 9:16

Nehemiah 9:11
[1]Lit *strong, mighty*
[a]Ex 14:21
[b]Ex 15:1, 5, 10

Nehemiah 9:12
[a]Ex 13:21, 22

Nehemiah 9:13
[a]Ex 19:11, 18-20
[b]Ex 20:1
[c]Ps 19:7-9

Nehemiah 9:14
[a]Ex 16:23; 20:8

Nehemiah 9:15
[1]Lit *lifted up Your hand*
[a]Ex 16:4, 14, 15
[b]Ex 17:6; Num 20:7-13
[c]Deut 1:8, 21

Nehemiah 9:16
[1]Lit *stiffened their neck;* so also v 17
[a]Neh 9:10
[b]Deut 1:26-33; 31:27; Neh 9:29

Nehemiah 9:17
[1]So Gr and some Heb mss; Heb reads *in their rebellion*
[a]Ps 78:11, 42-55
[b]Num 14:4
[c]Ex 34:6, 7; Num 14:18

Nehemiah 9:18
[1]Lit *acts of contempt*
[a]Ex 32:4-8, 31

Nehemiah 9:27
[a]Judg 2:14
[b]Deut 4:29
[c]Judg 2:16

Nehemiah 9:28
[a]Judg 3:11
[b]Ps 106:43

Nehemiah 9:29
[1]Lit *gave*
[a]Neh 9:26, 30
[b]Neh 9:10, 16
[c]Lev 18:5
[d]Zech 7:11

Nehemiah 9:30
[a]Ps 95:10; Acts 13:18
[b]2 Kin 17:13-18; 2 Chr 36:15, 16; Neh 9:26, 29
[c]Neh 9:20

Nehemiah 9:31
[a]Jer 4:27
[b]Neh 9:17

Nehemiah 9:32
[a]Neh 1:5
[b]2 Kin 15:19, 29; 2 Kin 17:3-6; Ezra 4:2, 10

Nehemiah 9:33
[a]Gen 18:25; Jer 12:1

Nehemiah 9:34
[1]Lit *testimonies*
[2]Or *witnessed*

Nehemiah 9:35
[a]Deut 28:47

	[b]Neh 9:25
	Nehemiah 9:36 [a]Deut 28:48
	Nehemiah 9:37 [a]Deut 28:33
	Nehemiah 9:38 [1]Ch 10:1 in Heb [a]Neh 10:29 [b]Neh 10:1

Process of Discovery

Linguistics Section

Linguistic Structure

[Introduction to the poetry] [1] Now on the twenty-fourth day of *[a]*this month the sons of Israel assembled *[b]*with fasting, in sackcloth and with *[c]*dirt upon them. [2] The [1a]descendants of Israel separated themselves from all foreigners, and stood and *[b]*confessed their sins and the iniquities of their fathers. [3] While *[a]*they stood in their place, they read from the book of the law of the LORD their God for a fourth of the day; and for *another* fourth they confessed and worshiped the LORD their God. [4] *[a]*Now on the Levites' platform stood Jeshua, Bani, Kadmiel, Shebaniah, Bunni, Sherebiah, Bani *and* Chenani, and they cried with a loud voice to the LORD their God.

[5] Then the Levites, Jeshua, Kadmiel, Bani, Hashabneiah, Sherebiah, Hodiah, Shebaniah *and* Pethahiah, said, "Arise, bless the LORD your God forever and ever!

[Prayer in Poetry]

O may Your glorious name be blessed
And exalted above all blessing and praise!
[6] "*[a]*You alone are the LORD.
*[b]*You have made the heavens,
The heaven of heavens with all their host,
The earth and all that is on it,
The seas and all that is in them.
*[c]*You give life to all of them
And the heavenly host bows down before You.
[7] "You are the LORD God,
*[a]*Who chose Abram
And brought him out from *[b]*Ur of the Chaldees,
And *[c]*gave him the name Abraham.
[8] "You found *[a]*his heart faithful before You,
And made a covenant with him
To give *him* the land of the Canaanite,
Of the Hittite and the Amorite,
Of the Perizzite, the Jebusite and the Girgashite —
To give *it* to his [1]descendants.
And You *[b]*have fulfilled Your promise,
For You are righteous.

[9] "*[a]*You saw the affliction of our fathers in Egypt,

And *b*heard their cry by the ¹Red Sea.

10 "Then You performed *a*signs and wonders against Pharaoh,
Against all his servants and all the people of his land;
For You knew that *b*they acted arrogantly toward them,
And *c*made a name for Yourself as *it is* this day.

11 "*a*You divided the sea before them,
So they passed through the midst of the sea on dry ground;
And *b*their pursuers You hurled into the depths,
Like a stone into ¹raging waters.

12 "And with a pillar of cloud *a*You led them by day,
And with a pillar of fire by night
To light for them the way
In which they were to go.

13 "Then *a*You came down on Mount Sinai,
And *b*spoke with them from heaven;
You gave them *c*just ordinances and true laws,
Good statutes and commandments.

14 "So You made known to them *a*Your holy sabbath,
And laid down for them commandments, statutes and law,
Through Your servant Moses.

15 "You *a*provided bread from heaven for them for their hunger,
You *b*brought forth water from a rock for them for their thirst,
And You *c*told them to enter in order to possess
The land which You ¹swore to give them.

16 "But they, our fathers, *a*acted arrogantly;
They ¹*b*became stubborn and would not listen to Your commandments.

17 "They refused to listen,
And *a*did not remember Your wondrous deeds which You had performed among them;
So they became stubborn and *b*appointed a leader to return to their slavery ¹in Egypt.
But You are a God *c*of forgiveness,
Gracious and compassionate,
Slow to anger and abounding in lovingkindness;
And You did not forsake them.

18 "Even when they *a*made for themselves
A calf of molten metal
And said, 'This is your God
Who brought you up from Egypt,'
And committed great ¹blasphemies,

19 ^a"You, in Your great compassion,
Did not forsake them in the wilderness;
^bThe pillar of cloud did not leave them by day,
To guide them on their way,
Nor the pillar of fire by night, to light for them the way in which they were to
go.

20 "^aYou gave Your good Spirit to instruct them,
Your manna You did not withhold from their mouth,
And You gave them water for their thirst.

21 "Indeed, ^aforty years You provided for them in the wilderness *and* they were
not in want;
Their clothes did not wear out, nor did their feet swell.

22 "You also gave them kingdoms and peoples,
And allotted *them* to them as a ¹boundary.
^aThey took possession of the land of Sihon ²the king of Heshbon
And the land of Og the king of Bashan.

23 "You made their sons numerous as ^athe stars of heaven,
And You brought them into the land
Which You had told their fathers to enter and possess.

24 "^aSo their sons entered and possessed the land.
And ^bYou subdued before them the inhabitants of the land, the Canaanites,
And You gave them into their hand, with their kings and the peoples of the
land,
To do with them ¹as they desired.

25 "^aThey captured fortified cities and a ^{1b}fertile land.
They took possession of ^chouses full of every good thing,
Hewn cisterns, vineyards, olive groves,
Fruit trees in abundance.
So they ate, were filled and ^dgrew fat,
And ^ereveled in Your great goodness.

26 "^aBut they became disobedient and rebelled against You,
And ^bcast Your law behind their backs
And ^ckilled Your prophets who had ^dadmonished them
So that they might return to You,
And ^ethey committed great ¹blasphemies.

27 "Therefore You ^adelivered them into the hand of their oppressors who
oppressed them,
But when they cried to You ^bin the time of their distress,
You heard from heaven, and according to Your great compassion

You [c]gave them deliverers who delivered them from the hand of their oppressors.

28 "But [a]as soon as they had rest, they did evil again before You;

Therefore You abandoned them to the hand of their enemies, so that they ruled over them.

When they cried again to You, You heard from heaven,

And [b]many times You rescued them according to Your compassion,

29 And [a]admonished them in order to turn them back to Your law.

Yet [b]they acted arrogantly and did not listen to Your commandments but sinned against Your ordinances,

By [c]which if a man observes them he shall live.

And they [1d]turned a stubborn shoulder and stiffened their neck, and would not listen.

30 "[a]However, You bore with them for many years,

And [b]admonished them by [c]Your Spirit through Your prophets,

Yet they would not give ear.

Therefore You gave them into the hand of the peoples of the lands.

31 "Nevertheless, in Your great compassion You [a]did not make an end of them or forsake them,

For You are [b]a gracious and compassionate God.

32 "Now therefore, our God, [a]the great, the mighty, and the awesome God, who keeps covenant and lovingkindness,

Do not let all the hardship seem insignificant before You,

Which has come upon us, our kings, our princes, our priests, our prophets, our fathers and on all Your people,

[b]From the days of the kings of Assyria to this day.

33 "However, [a]You are just in all that has come upon us;

For You have dealt faithfully, but we have acted wickedly.

34 "For our kings, our leaders, our priests and our fathers have not kept Your law

Or paid attention to Your commandments and Your [1]admonitions with which You have [2]admonished them.

35 "But [a]they, in their own kingdom,

[b]With Your great goodness which You gave them,

With the broad and rich land which You set before them,

Did not serve You or turn from their evil deeds.

36 "Behold, [a]we are slaves today,

And as to the land which You gave to our fathers to eat of its fruit and its bounty,

Behold, we are slaves in it.

37 "[a]Its abundant produce is for the kings

Whom You have set over us because of our sins;
They also rule over our bodies
And over our cattle as they please,
So we are in great distress.

38   "¹Now because of all this
*We are making an agreement in writing;
And on the *sealed document *are the names of* our leaders, our Levites *and* our

priests."

Discussion

This chapter is composed of a poetic pray that was offered to the people by several Levites. The fasting and prayer was an experience of the High Holiday worship (Rosh HaShannah and Yom Kippur). There is a passionate call for repentance and confession of sin. It also offers a Scriptural view of human events as the LORD moved the Jewish people through history.[36]

Questioning the Passage

1. What day is referred to in verse one?

    The month was Tishrei. On the twenty-fourth day, the people gathered for a time of fasting and repentance prayer. The Levites had to wait until the 24th day of the month because fasting is forbidden at Festivals. Succot is celeberated in Tishrei.

2. Why did the people fast? (v. 1)

    Fasting represents the denial of one's desires and the bitterness of one's heart.[37]

---

[36] Nosson Scherman and Meir Zlotowitz, *The Writings = Kesuvim / The Writings: with a Commentary Anthologized from Rabbinic Writings = Ketuvim: 'im Perush Rashi, Metsudat David, Metsudat Tsiyon, ye-'od* (Brooklyn, NY: Mesorah Publications, 2016).
[37] IBID.

3. What is the "law of the LORD?" (v. 3)

   This is a reference to the Torah.

4. Why is the history of the LORD's interaction with Israel offered?

   The people were reminded of how the LORD selected their ancestor Abraham and made them a nation that started with him. The LORD always protects the nation of Israel. Even when the people sinned against the LORD, the LORD was them. The brief history lesson was to remind the people of the love and power of the LORD.

Biblical Personalities

1. Jeshua, Bani, Kadmiel, Shebaniah, Bunni, Sherebiah, Bani *and* Chenani. These were the Levites who stood on the platform and told the people about their

Thoughts

The idea of reviewing history to see how the promises and covenants of the LORD have been maintained even when we sin is not often done today. If today's people forget their history, they are doomed to repeat past mistakes. The Levites wanted to remind the people that the LORD has always been with them. They needed to return to Adonai-worship. Why? Because throughout their history, Adonai was with the people. It is also a rallying cry to keep the people together.

Chapter Ten

Language

New American Standard 1995	Hebrew
Neh. 10:1 [1]Now on the [a]sealed document *were the names of:* Nehemiah the [2]governor, the son of Hacaliah, and Zedekiah, [2] Seraiah, Azariah, Jeremiah, [3] Pashhur, Amariah, Malchijah, [4] Hattush, Shebaniah, Malluch, [5] Harim, Meremoth, Obadiah, [6] Daniel, Ginnethon, Baruch, [7] Meshullam, Abijah, Mijamin, [8] Maaziah, Bilgai, Shemaiah. These *were* the priests. [9] And the Levites: Jeshua the son of Azaniah, Binnui of the sons of Henadad, Kadmiel; [10] also their brothers Shebaniah, Hodiah, Kelita, Pelaiah, Hanan, [11] Mica, Rehob, Hashabiah, [12] Zaccur, Sherebiah, Shebaniah, [13] Hodiah, Bani, Beninu. [14] The leaders of the people: Parosh, Pahath-moab, Elam, Zattu, Bani, [15] Bunni, Azgad, Bebai, [16] Adonijah, Bigvai, Adin, [17] Ater, Hezekiah, Azzur, [18] Hodiah, Hashum, Bezai, [19] Hariph, Anathoth, Nebai, [20] Magpiash, Meshullam, Hezir, [21] Meshezabel, Zadok, Jaddua, [22] Pelatiah, Hanan, Anaiah, [23] Hoshea, Hananiah, Hasshub, [24] Hallohesh, Pilha, Shobek, [25] Rehum, Hashabnah, Maaseiah, [26] Ahiah, Hanan, Anan, [27] Malluch, Harim, Baanah. **Neh. 10:28** Now [a]the rest of the people, the priests, the Levites, the gatekeepers, the singers, the temple servants and [b]all those who had separated themselves from the peoples of the lands to the law of God, their wives, their sons and their daughters, all those who had knowledge and understanding, [29] are joining with their [1]kinsmen, their nobles, and are	Neh. 10:1 וּבְכָל־זֹאת אֲנַחְנוּ כֹּרְתִים אֲמָנָה וְכֹתְבִים וְעַל הֶחָתוּם שָׂרֵינוּ לְוִיֵּנוּ כֹּהֲנֵינוּ: [2] וְעַל הַחֲתוּמִים נְחֶמְיָה הַתִּרְשָׁתָא בֶּן־חֲכַלְיָה וְצִדְקִיָּה: [3] שְׂרָיָה עֲזַרְיָה יִרְמְיָה: [4] פַּשְׁחוּר אֲמַרְיָה מַלְכִּיָּה: [5] חַטּוּשׁ שְׁבַנְיָה מַלּוּךְ: [6] חָרִם מְרֵמוֹת עֹבַדְיָה: [7] דָּנִיֵּאל גִּנְּתוֹן בָּרוּךְ: [8] מְשֻׁלָּם אֲבִיָּה מִיָּמִן: [9] מַעַזְיָה בִלְגַּי שְׁמַעְיָה אֵלֶּה הַכֹּהֲנִים: ס [10] וְהַלְוִיִּם וְיֵשׁוּעַ בֶּן־אֲזַנְיָה בִּנּוּי מִבְּנֵי חֵנָדָד קַדְמִיאֵל: [11] וַאֲחֵיהֶם שְׁבַנְיָה הוֹדִיָּה קְלִיטָא פְּלָאיָה חָנָן: [12] מִיכָא רְחוֹב חֲשַׁבְיָה: [13] זַכּוּר שֵׁרֵבְיָה שְׁבַנְיָה: [14] הוֹדִיָּה בָנִי בְּנִינוּ: ס [15] רָאשֵׁי הָעָם פַּרְעֹשׁ פַּחַת מוֹאָב עֵילָם זַתּוּא בָּנִי: [16] בֻּנִּי עַזְגָּד בֵּבָי: [17] אֲדֹנִיָּה בִגְוַי עָדִין: [18] אָטֵר חִזְקִיָּה עַזּוּר: [19] הוֹדִיָּה חָשֻׁם בֵּצָי: [20] חָרִיף עֲנָתוֹת נוֹבָי [נֵיבָי:] [21] מַגְפִּיעָשׁ מְשֻׁלָּם חֵזִיר: [22] מְשֵׁיזַבְאֵל צָדוֹק יַדּוּעַ: [23] פְּלַטְיָה חָנָן עֲנָיָה: [24] הוֹשֵׁעַ חֲנַנְיָה חַשּׁוּב: [25] הַלּוֹחֵשׁ פִּלְחָא שׁוֹבֵק: [26] רְחוּם חֲשַׁבְנָה מַעֲשֵׂיָה: [27] וַאֲחִיָּה חָנָן עָנָן: [28]

[2a]taking on themselves a curse and an oath to walk in God's law, which was given through Moses, God's servant, and to keep and to observe all the commandments of [3]GOD our Lord, and His ordinances and His statutes; [30] and [a]that we will not give our daughters to the peoples of the land or take their daughters for our sons. [31] As [a]for the peoples of the land who bring wares or any grain on the sabbath day to sell, we will not buy from them on the sabbath or a holy day; and we will forego *the crops* the [b]seventh year and the [c]exaction of every debt.

Neh. 10:32 We also [1]placed ourselves under obligation to contribute yearly [a]one third of a shekel for the service of the house of our God: [33] for the [a]showbread, for the continual grain offering, for the continual burnt offering, the sabbaths, the new moon, for the appointed times, for the holy things and for the sin offerings to make atonement for Israel, and all the work of the house of our God.

Neh. 10:34 Likewise [a]we cast lots [b]for the supply of wood *among* the priests, the Levites and the people so that they might bring it to the house of our God, according to our fathers' households, at fixed times annually, to burn on the altar of the LORD our God, as it is written in the law; [35] and that they might bring the first fruits of our ground and [a]the first fruits of all the fruit of every tree to the house of the LORD annually, [36] and [a]bring to the house of our God the firstborn of our sons and of our cattle, and the firstborn of our herds and our

מָלוֹךְ חָרִם בַּעֲנָה: 29 וּשְׁאָר הָעָם
הַכֹּהֲנִים הַלְוִיִּם הַשּׁוֹעֲרִים
הַמְשֹׁרְרִים הַנְּתִינִים וְכָל־הַנִּבְדָּל
מֵעַמֵּי הָאֲרָצוֹת אֶל־תּוֹרַת
הָאֱלֹהִים נְשֵׁיהֶם בְּנֵיהֶם וּבְנֹתֵיהֶם
כֹּל יוֹדֵעַ מֵבִין: 30 מַחֲזִיקִים עַל־
אֲחֵיהֶם אַדִּירֵיהֶם וּבָאִים בְּאָלָה
וּבִשְׁבוּעָה לָלֶכֶת בְּתוֹרַת הָאֱלֹהִים
אֲשֶׁר נִתְּנָה בְּיַד מֹשֶׁה עֶבֶד־
הָאֱלֹהִים וְלִשְׁמוֹר וְלַעֲשׂוֹת אֶת־
כָּל־מִצְוֹת יְהוָה אֲדֹנֵינוּ וּמִשְׁפָּטָיו
וְחֻקָּיו: 31 וַאֲשֶׁר לֹא־נִתֵּן בְּנֹתֵינוּ
לְעַמֵּי הָאָרֶץ וְאֶת־בְּנֹתֵיהֶם לֹא
נִקַּח לְבָנֵינוּ: 32 וְעַמֵּי הָאָרֶץ
הַמְבִיאִים אֶת־הַמַּקָּחוֹת וְכָל־שֶׁבֶר
בְּיוֹם הַשַּׁבָּת לִמְכּוֹר לֹא־נִקַּח מֵהֶם
בַּשַּׁבָּת וּבְיוֹם קֹדֶשׁ וְנִטֹּשׁ אֶת־
הַשָּׁנָה הַשְּׁבִיעִית וּמַשָּׁא כָל־יָד: 33
וְהֶעֱמַדְנוּ עָלֵינוּ מִצְוֹת לָתֵת עָלֵינוּ
שְׁלִשִׁית הַשֶּׁקֶל בַּשָּׁנָה לַעֲבֹדַת בֵּית
אֱלֹהֵינוּ: 34 לְלֶחֶם הַמַּעֲרֶכֶת
וּמִנְחַת הַתָּמִיד וּלְעוֹלַת הַתָּמִיד
הַשַּׁבָּתוֹת הֶחֳדָשִׁים לַמּוֹעֲדִים
וְלַקֳּדָשִׁים וְלַחַטָּאוֹת לְכַפֵּר עַל־
יִשְׂרָאֵל וְכֹל מְלֶאכֶת בֵּית־
אֱלֹהֵינוּ: ס 35 וְהַגּוֹרָלוֹת הִפַּלְנוּ
עַל־קֻרְבַּן הָעֵצִים הַכֹּהֲנִים הַלְוִיִּם
וְהָעָם לְהָבִיא לְבֵית אֱלֹהֵינוּ

flocks as it is written in the law, for the priests who are ministering in the house of our God. [37] *We will also bring the first of our [1]dough, our contributions, the fruit of every tree, the new wine and the oil [b]to the priests at the chambers of the house of our God, and the [c]tithe of our ground to the Levites, for the Levites are they who receive the tithes in all the rural towns. [38] *The priest, the son of Aaron, shall be with the Levites when the Levites receive tithes, and the Levites shall bring up the tenth of the tithes to the house of our God, to the chambers of [b]the storehouse. [39] For the sons of Israel and the sons of Levi shall bring the [a]contribution of the grain, the new wine and the oil to the chambers; there are the utensils of the sanctuary, the priests who are ministering, the gatekeepers and the singers. Thus [b]we will not [1]neglect the house of our God.

לְבֵית־אֲבֹתֵינוּ לְעִתִּים מְזֻמָּנִים שָׁנָה בְשָׁנָה לְבַעֵר עַל־מִזְבַּח יְהוָה אֱלֹהֵינוּ כַּכָּתוּב בַּתּוֹרָה׃ 36 וּלְהָבִיא אֶת־בִּכּוּרֵי אַדְמָתֵנוּ וּבִכּוּרֵי כָל־פְּרִי כָל־עֵץ שָׁנָה בְשָׁנָה לְבֵית יְהוָה׃ 37 וְאֶת־בְּכֹרוֹת בָּנֵינוּ וּבְהֶמְתֵּינוּ כַּכָּתוּב בַּתּוֹרָה וְאֶת־בְּכוֹרֵי בְקָרֵינוּ וְצֹאנֵינוּ לְהָבִיא לְבֵית אֱלֹהֵינוּ לַכֹּהֲנִים הַמְשָׁרְתִים בְּבֵית אֱלֹהֵינוּ׃ 38 וְאֶת־רֵאשִׁית עֲרִיסֹתֵינוּ וּתְרוּמֹתֵינוּ וּפְרִי כָל־עֵץ תִּירוֹשׁ וְיִצְהָר נָבִיא לַכֹּהֲנִים אֶל־לִשְׁכוֹת בֵּית־אֱלֹהֵינוּ וּמַעְשַׂר אַדְמָתֵנוּ לַלְוִיִּם וְהֵם הַלְוִיִּם הַמְעַשְּׂרִים בְּכֹל עָרֵי עֲבֹדָתֵנוּ׃ 39 וְהָיָה הַכֹּהֵן בֶּן־אַהֲרֹן עִם־הַלְוִיִּם בַּעְשֵׂר הַלְוִיִּם וְהַלְוִיִּם יַעֲלוּ אֶת־מַעֲשַׂר הַמַּעֲשֵׂר לְבֵית אֱלֹהֵינוּ אֶל־הַלְּשָׁכוֹת לְבֵית הָאוֹצָר׃ 40 כִּי אֶל־הַלְּשָׁכוֹת יָבִיאוּ בְנֵי־יִשְׂרָאֵל וּבְנֵי הַלֵּוִי אֶת־תְּרוּמַת הַדָּגָן הַתִּירוֹשׁ וְהַיִּצְהָר וְשָׁם כְּלֵי הַמִּקְדָּשׁ וְהַכֹּהֲנִים הַמְשָׁרְתִים וְהַשּׁוֹעֲרִים וְהַמְשֹׁרְרִים וְלֹא נַעֲזֹב אֶת־בֵּית אֱלֹהֵינוּ׃

References

<table>
<tr><td>

Nehemiah 10:1
[1]Ch 10:2 in Heb
[2]Heb *Tirshatha,* a Persian title
[a]Neh 9:38

Nehemiah 10:28
[a]Ezra 2:36-58
[b]Neh 9:2

Nehemiah 10:29
[1]Lit *brothers*
[2]Lit *entering into a*
[3]Heb *YHWH,* usually rendered *LORD*
[a]Neh 5:12

Nehemiah 10:30
[a]Ex 34:16; Deut 7:3

Nehemiah 10:31
[a]Neh 13:15-22
[b]Ex 23:10, 11; Lev 25:1-7
[c]Deut 15:1, 2

Nehemiah 10:32
[1]Lit *imposed commandments on us*
[a]Ex 30:11-16; Matt 17:24

</td><td>

Nehemiah 10:33
[a]Lev 24:5, 6; 2 Chr 2:4

Nehemiah 10:34
[a]Neh 11:1
[b]Neh 13:31

Nehemiah 10:35
[a]Ex 23:19; 34:26; Deut 26:2

Nehemiah 10:36
[a]Ex 13:2

Nehemiah 10:37
[1]Or *coarse meal*
[a]Lev 23:17
[b]Neh 13:5, 9
[c]Lev 27:30; Num 18:21

Nehemiah 10:38
[a]Num 18:26
[b]Neh 13:12, 13

Nehemiah 10:39
[1]Lit *forsake*
[a]Deut 12:6
[b]Neh 13:10, 11

</td></tr>
</table>

Process of Discovery

Linguistics Section

Linguistic Structure

[The Sealed Document] [1]Now on the [a]sealed document *were the names of:* Nehemiah the [2]governor, the son of Hacaliah, and Zedekiah, [2] Seraiah, Azariah, Jeremiah, [3] Pashhur, Amariah, Malchijah, [4] Hattush, Shebaniah, Malluch, [5] Harim, Meremoth, Obadiah, [6] Daniel, Ginnethon, Baruch, [7] Meshullam, Abijah, Mijamin, [8] Maaziah, Bilgai, Shemaiah. These *were* the priests. [9] And the Levites: Jeshua the son of Azaniah, Binnui of the sons of Henadad, Kadmiel; [10] also their brothers Shebaniah, Hodiah, Kelita, Pelaiah, Hanan, [11] Mica, Rehob, Hashabiah, [12] Zaccur, Sherebiah, Shebaniah, [13] Hodiah, Bani, Beninu. [14] The leaders of the people: Parosh, Pahath-moab, Elam, Zattu, Bani, [15] Bunni, Azgad, Bebai, [16] Adonijah, Bigvai, Adin, [17] Ater, Hezekiah, Azzur, [18] Hodiah, Hashum, Bezai, [19] Hariph, Anathoth, Nebai, [20] Magpiash, Meshullam, Hezir, [21] Meshezabel, Zadok, Jaddua, [22] Pelatiah, Hanan, Anaiah, [23] Hoshea, Hananiah, Hasshub, [24] Hallohesh, Pilha, Shobek, [25] Rehum, Hashabnah, Maaseiah, [26] Ahiah, Hanan, Anan, [27] Malluch, Harim, Baanah.

[The rest of the people] [28] Now [a]the rest of the people, the priests, the Levites, the gatekeepers, the singers, the temple servants and [b]all those who had separated themselves from the peoples of the lands to the law of God, their wives, their sons and their daughters, all those who had knowledge and understanding, [29] are joining with their [1]kinsmen, their nobles, and are [2a]taking on themselves a curse and an oath to walk in God's law, which was given through Moses, God's servant, and to keep and to observe all the commandments of [3]GOD our Lord, and His ordinances and His statutes; [30] and [a]that we will not give our daughters to the peoples of the land or take their daughters for our sons. [31] As [a]for the peoples of the land who bring wares or any grain on the sabbath day to sell, we will not buy from them on the sabbath or a holy day; and we will forego *the crops* the [b]seventh year and the [c]exaction of every debt.

[Yearly contribution] [32] We also [1]placed ourselves under obligation to contribute yearly [a]one third of a shekel for the service of the house of our God: [33] for the [a]showbread, for the continual grain offering, for the continual burnt offering, the sabbaths, the new moon, for the appointed times, for the holy things and for the sin offerings to make atonement for Israel, and all the work of the house of our God.

[A Covenent] Likewise [a]we cast lots [b]for the supply of wood *among* the priests, the Levites and the people so that they might bring it to the house of our God, according to our fathers' households, at fixed times annually, to burn on the altar of the LORD our God, as it is written in the law; [35] and that they might bring the first fruits of our ground and *the first fruits of all the fruit of every tree to the house of the LORD annually, **36** and *bring to the house of our God the firstborn of our sons and of our cattle, and the firstborn of our herds and our flocks as it is written in the law, for the priests who are ministering in the house of our God. **37** *We will also bring the first of our ¹dough, our contributions, the fruit of every tree, the new wine and the oil *to the priests at the chambers of the house of our God, and the *tithe of our ground to the Levites, for the Levites are they who receive the tithes in all the rural towns. **38** *The priest, the son of Aaron, shall be with the Levites when the Levites receive tithes, and the Levites shall bring up the tenth of the tithes to the house of our God, to the chambers of *the storehouse. **39** For the sons of Israel and the sons of Levi shall bring the *contribution of the grain, the new wine and the oil to the chambers; there are the utensils of the sanctuary, the priests who are ministering, the gatekeepers and the singers. Thus *we will not ¹neglect the house of our God.

Discussion

This chapter outlines a document that was signed by the people to serve the LORD. The tithe from the people is defined. Nehemiah knew how much income he needed to rebuild the Temple. This chapter shows that the people were dedicated to the work. They willingly gave of the LORD's graces to the rebuilding of His Temple.

Thoughts

The people came forward and gave what was needed for the rebuilding of the Temple. I was the lead pastor at a church that wanted to build an addition. There was an incredible amount of resistance to this idea. Why? Simply put, about 15% of the people did not want to make a sacrificial donation to the church. Except for one couple, all of the detractors left the church. The 15% came to the decisive vote and told the 85% that the LORD told them not to build the building. The 85% said that the LORD told them to build it. Imagine what would have happened in Jerusalem under Nehemiah's rule if this would have happened? Nehemiah would have been recalled, and someone else would have assumed the leadership role. If the LORD wants something done, He will put a leader in charge who will get it done.

Chapter Eleven

Language

New American Standard 1995	Hebrew
Neh. 11:1 Now [a]the leaders of the people lived in Jerusalem, but the rest of the people [b]cast lots to bring one out of ten to live in Jerusalem, [c]the holy city, while nine-tenths *remained* in the *other* cities. [2] And the people blessed all the men who [a]volunteered to live in Jerusalem. **Neh. 11:3** [a]Now these are the heads of the provinces who lived in Jerusalem, but in the cities of Judah [b]each lived on his own property in their cities — the [1]Israelites, the priests, the Levites, the [2c]temple servants and the [3d]descendants of Solomon's servants. [4] Some of the sons of Judah and some of the sons of Benjamin lived in Jerusalem. From the sons of Judah: Athaiah the son of Uzziah, the son of Zechariah, the son of Amariah, the son of Shephatiah, the son of Mahalalel, of the sons of Perez; [5] and Maaseiah the son of Baruch, the son of Col-hozeh, the son of Hazaiah, the son of Adaiah, the son of Joiarib, the son of Zechariah, the son of the Shilonite. [6] All the sons of Perez who lived in Jerusalem were 468 able men. **Neh. 11:7** Now these are the sons of Benjamin: Sallu the son of Meshullam, the son of Joed, the son of Pedaiah, the son of Kolaiah, the son of Maaseiah, the	וַיֵּשְׁבוּ שָׂרֵי־הָעָם בִּירוּשָׁלִָם Neh. 11:1 וּשְׁאָר הָעָם הִפִּילוּ גוֹרָלוֹת לְהָבִיא אֶחָד מִן־הָעֲשָׂרָה לָשֶׁבֶת בִּירוּשָׁלִַם עִיר הַקֹּדֶשׁ וְתֵשַׁע הַיָּדוֹת בֶּעָרִים: 2 וַיְבָרֲכוּ הָעָם לְכֹל הָאֲנָשִׁים הַמִּתְנַדְּבִים לָשֶׁבֶת בִּירוּשָׁלִָם: פ 3 וְאֵלֶּה רָאשֵׁי הַמְּדִינָה אֲשֶׁר יָשְׁבוּ בִּירוּשָׁלִָם וּבְעָרֵי יְהוּדָה יָשְׁבוּ אִישׁ בַּאֲחֻזָּתוֹ בְּעָרֵיהֶם יִשְׂרָאֵל הַכֹּהֲנִים וְהַלְוִיִּם וְהַנְּתִינִים וּבְנֵי עַבְדֵי שְׁלֹמֹה: 4 וּבִירוּשָׁלִַם יָשְׁבוּ מִבְּנֵי יְהוּדָה וּמִבְּנֵי בִנְיָמִן מִבְּנֵי יְהוּדָה עֲתָיָה בֶן־עֻזִּיָּה בֶּן־זְכַרְיָה בֶּן־אֲמַרְיָה בֶּן־ שְׁפַטְיָה בֶּן־מַהֲלַלְאֵל מִבְּנֵי־פָרֶץ: 5 וּמַעֲשֵׂיָה בֶן־בָּרוּךְ בֶּן־כָּל־חֹזֶה בֶּן־חֲזָיָה בֶן־עֲדָיָה בֶן־יוֹיָרִיב בֶּן־ זְכַרְיָה בֶּן־הַשִּׁלֹנִי: 6 כָּל־בְּנֵי־פֶרֶץ הַיֹּשְׁבִים בִּירוּשָׁלִָם אַרְבַּע מֵאוֹת שִׁשִּׁים וּשְׁמֹנָה אַנְשֵׁי־חָיִל: ס 7 וְאֵלֶּה בְּנֵי בִנְיָמִן סַלֻּא בֶּן־מְשֻׁלָּם בֶּן־יוֹעֵד בֶּן־פְּדָיָה בֶּן־קוֹלָיָה בֶּן־ מַעֲשֵׂיָה בֶּן־אִיתִיאֵל בֶּן־יְשַׁעְיָה: 8

son of Ithiel, the son of Jeshaiah; [8] and after him Gabbai *and* Sallai, 928. [9] Joel the son of Zichri was their overseer, and Judah the son of Hassenuah was second [1]in command of the city.

Neh. 11:10   From the priests: Jedaiah the son of Joiarib, Jachin, [11] Seraiah the son of Hilkiah, the son of Meshullam, the son of Zadok, the son of Meraioth, the son of Ahitub, the leader of the house of God, [12] and their [1]kinsmen who performed the work of the [2]temple, 822; and Adaiah the son of Jeroham, the son of Pelaliah, the son of Amzi, the son of Zechariah, the son of Pashhur, the son of Malchijah, [13] and his kinsmen, heads of fathers' *households,* 242; and Amashsai the son of Azarel, the son of Ahzai, the son of Meshillemoth, the son of Immer, [14] and their brothers, valiant warriors, 128. And their overseer was Zabdiel, the son of [1]Haggedolim.

Neh. 11:15   Now from the Levites: Shemaiah the son of Hasshub, the son of Azrikam, the son of Hashabiah, the son of Bunni; [16] and Shabbethai and Jozabad, from the [1]leaders of the Levites, who were [2]in charge of [a]the outside work of the house of God; [17] and Mattaniah the son of Mica, the son of [1]Zabdi, the son of Asaph, who was the [2]leader in beginning the thanksgiving at prayer, and Bakbukiah, the second among his brethren; and [3]Abda the son of [4]Shammua, the son of Galal, the son of Jeduthun. [18] All the Levites in [a]the holy city *were* 284.

וְאַחֲרָיו גַּבַּי סַלָּי תְּשַׁע מֵאוֹת עֶשְׂרִים וּשְׁמֹנָה : [9] וְיוֹאֵל בֶּן־זִכְרִי פָּקִיד עֲלֵיהֶם וִיהוּדָה בֶן־הַסְּנוּאָה עַל־הָעִיר מִשְׁנֶה : פ [10] מִן־הַכֹּהֲנִים יְדַעְיָה בֶן־יוֹיָרִיב יָכִין : [11] שְׂרָיָה בֶן־חִלְקִיָּה בֶּן־מְשֻׁלָּם בֶּן־צָדוֹק בֶּן־מְרָיוֹת בֶּן־אֲחִיטוּב נְגִד בֵּית הָאֱלֹהִים : [12] וַאֲחֵיהֶם עֹשֵׂי הַמְּלָאכָה לַבַּיִת שְׁמֹנָה מֵאוֹת עֶשְׂרִים וּשְׁנָיִם וַעֲדָיָה בֶּן־יְרֹחָם בֶּן־פְּלַלְיָה בֶּן־אַמְצִי בֶּן־זְכַרְיָה בֶּן־פַּשְׁחוּר בֶּן־מַלְכִּיָּה : [13] וְאֶחָיו רָאשִׁים לְאָבוֹת מָאתַיִם אַרְבָּעִים וּשְׁנָיִם וַעֲמַשְׁסַי בֶּן־עֲזַרְאֵל בֶּן־אַחְזַי בֶּן־מְשִׁלֵּמוֹת בֶּן־אִמֵּר : [14] וַאֲחֵיהֶם גִּבּוֹרֵי חַיִל מֵאָה עֶשְׂרִים וּשְׁמֹנָה וּפָקִיד עֲלֵיהֶם זַבְדִּיאֵל בֶּן־הַגְּדוֹלִים : ס [15] וּמִן־הַלְוִיִּם שְׁמַעְיָה בֶן־חַשּׁוּב בֶּן־עַזְרִיקָם בֶּן־חֲשַׁבְיָה בֶּן־בּוּנִּי : [16] וְשַׁבְּתַי וְיוֹזָבָד עַל־הַמְּלָאכָה הַחִיצֹנָה לְבֵית הָאֱלֹהִים מֵרָאשֵׁי הַלְוִיִּם : [17] וּמַתַּנְיָה בֶן־מִיכָה בֶּן־זַבְדִּי בֶּן־אָסָף רֹאשׁ הַתְּחִלָּה יְהוֹדֶה לַתְּפִלָּה וּבַקְבֻּקְיָה מִשְׁנֶה מֵאֶחָיו וְעַבְדָּא בֶּן־שַׁמּוּעַ בֶּן־גָּלָל בֶּן־יְדִיתוּן [יְדוּתוּן] : [18] כָּל־הַלְוִיִּם בְּעִיר הַקֹּדֶשׁ מָאתַיִם שְׁמֹנִים וְאַרְבָּעָה : פ [19] וְהַשּׁוֹעֲרִים

Neh. 11:19 Also the gatekeepers, Akkub, Talmon and their brethren who kept watch at the gates, *were* 172. [20] The rest of Israel, of the priests *and* of the Levites, *were* in all the cities of Judah, each [a]on his own inheritance. [21] But [a]the temple servants were living in Ophel, and Ziha and Gishpa were [1]in charge of the temple servants.

Neh. 11:22 Now [a]the overseer of the Levites in Jerusalem was Uzzi the son of Bani, the son of Hashabiah, the son of Mattaniah, the son of Mica, from the sons of Asaph, who were the singers for the [1]service of the house of God. [23] [a]For *there was* a commandment from the king concerning them and a firm regulation for the song leaders [b]day by day. [24] Pethahiah the son of Meshezabel, of the sons [a]of Zerah the son of Judah, was the [b]king's [1]representative in all matters concerning the people.

Neh. 11:25 Now as for the villages with their fields, some of the sons of Judah lived in [a]Kiriath-arba and its [1]towns, in [b]Dibon and its [1]towns, and in Jekabzeel and its villages, [26] and in Jeshua, in Moladah and Beth-pelet, [27] and in Hazar-shual, in Beersheba and its towns, [28] and in Ziklag, in Meconah and in its towns, [29] and in En-rimmon, in Zorah and in Jarmuth, [30] Zanoah, Adullam, and their villages, Lachish and its fields, Azekah and its towns. So they encamped from Beersheba as far as the valley of Hinnom. [31] The sons of Benjamin also *lived* from Geba *onward,* at Michmash and Aija, at Bethel and its towns, [32] at Anathoth, Nob, Ananiah, [33] Hazor, Ramah, Gittaim, [34]

עֲק֣וּב טַלְמ֔וֹן וַאֲחֵיהֶ֖ם הַשֹּׁמְרִ֑ים
בַּשְּׁעָרִ֕ים מֵאָ֖ה שִׁבְעִ֥ים וּשְׁנָֽיִם׃ [20] וּשְׁאָ֣ר יִשְׂרָאֵ֗ל הַכֹּהֲנִ֣ים הַלְוִיִּ֔ם בְּכָל־עָרֵ֖י יְהוּדָ֑ה אִ֖ישׁ בְּנַחֲלָתֽוֹ׃ [21] וְהַנְּתִינִ֖ים יֹשְׁבִ֣ים בָּעֹ֑פֶל וְצִיחָ֣א וְגִשְׁפָּ֔א עַל־הַנְּתִינִֽים׃ פ [22] וּפְקִ֤יד הַלְוִיִּם֙ בִּיר֣וּשָׁלִַ֔ם עֻזִּ֤י בֶן־בָּנִי֙ בֶּן־חֲשַׁבְיָ֔ה בֶּן־מַתַּנְיָ֖ה בֶּן־מִיכָ֑א מִבְּנֵ֣י אָסָ֗ף הַמְשֹׁרְרִים֙ לְנֶ֣גֶד מְלֶ֣אכֶת בֵּית־הָאֱלֹהִֽים׃ [23] כִּֽי־מִצְוַ֥ת הַמֶּ֖לֶךְ עֲלֵיהֶ֑ם וַאֲמָנָ֛ה עַל־הַמְשֹׁרְרִ֖ים דְּבַר־י֥וֹם בְּיוֹמֽוֹ׃ [24] וּפְתַֽחְיָ֨ה בֶּן־מְשֵֽׁיזַבְאֵ֜ל מִבְּנֵי־זֶ֤רַח בֶּן־יְהוּדָה֙ לְיַ֣ד הַמֶּ֔לֶךְ לְכָל־דָּבָ֖ר לָעָֽם׃ [25] וְאֶל־הַחֲצֵרִ֖ים בִּשְׂדֹתָ֑ם מִבְּנֵ֣י יְהוּדָ֗ה יָֽשְׁבוּ֙ בְּקִרְיַ֣ת הָֽאַרְבַּ֔ע וּבְנֹתֶ֕יהָ וּבְדִיבֹ֖ן וּבְנֹתֶ֑יהָ וּבִֽיקַּבְצְאֵ֖ל וַחֲצֵרֶֽיהָ׃ [26] וּבְיֵשׁ֥וּעַ וּבְמוֹלָדָ֖ה וּבְבֵ֥ית פָּֽלֶט׃ [27] וּבַחֲצַ֥ר שׁוּעָ֛ל וּבִבְאֵ֥ר שֶׁ֖בַע וּבְנֹתֶֽיהָ׃ [28] וּבְצִֽקְלַ֥ג וּבִמְכֹנָ֖ה וּבִבְנֹתֶֽיהָ׃ [29] וּבְעֵ֥ין רִמּ֛וֹן וּבְצָרְעָ֖ה וּבְיַרְמֽוּת׃ [30] זָנֹ֤חַ עֲדֻלָּם֙ וְחַצְרֵיהֶ֔ם לָכִ֥ישׁ וּשְׂדֹתֶ֖יהָ עֲזֵקָ֣ה וּבְנֹתֶ֑יהָ וַיַּחֲנ֥וּ מִבְּאֵֽר־שֶׁ֖בַע עַד־גֵּֽיא־הִנֹּֽם׃ [31] וּבְנֵ֣י בִנְיָמִ֗ן מִגֶּ֙בַע֙ מִכְמָ֣שׂ וְעַיָּ֔ה וּבֵֽית־אֵ֖ל וּבְנֹתֶֽיהָ׃ [32] עֲנָת֥וֹת נֹ֖ב עֲנָֽנְיָֽה׃ [33] חָצ֥וֹר ׀ רָמָ֖ה גִּתָּֽיִם׃ [34] חָדִ֥יד

<table>
<tr>
<td>

Hadid, Zeboim, Neballat, [35] Lod and Ono, the valley of craftsmen. [36] From the Levites, *some* divisions in Judah belonged to Benjamin.

</td>
<td dir="rtl">

צְבֹעִים נְבַלָּט: 35 לֹד וְאוֹנֹו גֵּי הַחֲרָשִׁים: 36 וּמִן־הַלְוִיִּם מַחְלְקוֹת יְהוּדָה לְבִנְיָמִין: פ

</td>
</tr>
</table>

References

Nehemiah 11:1
[a]Neh 7:4
[b]Neh 10:34
[c]Neh 11:18; Is 48:2

Nehemiah 11:2
[a]Judg 5:9

Nehemiah 11:3
[1]Lit *Israel*
[2]Heb *Nethinim*
[3]Lit *sons*
[a]1 Chr 9:2-34
[b]Neh 7:73; 11:20
[c]Ezra 2:43
[d]Neh 7:57

Nehemiah 11:9
[1]Lit *over*

Nehemiah 11:12
[1]Lit *brothers*, and so throughout the ch
[2]Lit *house*

Nehemiah 11:14
[1]Or *the great ones*

Nehemiah 11:16
[1]Lit *heads*
[2]Lit *over*
[a]1 Chr 26:29

Nehemiah 11:17
[1]In 1 Chr 9:15, *Zichri*
[2]Lit *head*
[3]In 1 Chr 9:16, *Obadiah*
[4]In 1 Chr 9:16, *Shemaiah*

Nehemiah 11:18
[a]Neh 11:1

Nehemiah 11:20
[a]Neh 11:3

Nehemiah 11:21
[1]Lit *over*
[a]Neh 3:26

Nehemiah 11:22
[1]Or *work*
[a]Neh 11:9, 14

Nehemiah 11:23
[a]Ezra 6:8; 7:20
[b]Neh 12:47

Nehemiah 11:24
[1]Lit *hand*
[a]Gen 38:30
[b]1 Chr 18:17

Nehemiah 11:25
[1]Lit *daughters*, and so throughout the ch
[a]Josh 14:15
[b]Josh 13:9, 17

Process of Discovery

Linguistics Section

Linguistic Structure

[Plan to bring people into the city] [1]   Now *a*the leaders of the people lived in Jerusalem, but the rest of the people *b*cast lots to bring one out of ten to live in Jerusalem, *c*the holy city, while nine-tenths *remained* in the *other* cities. [2] And the people blessed all the men who *a*volunteered to live in Jerusalem.

[Leaders in Jerusalem] [3]   *a*Now these are the heads of the provinces who lived in Jerusalem, but in the cities of Judah *b*each lived on his own property in their cities — the [1]Israelites, the priests, the Levites, the [2c]temple servants and the [3d]descendants of Solomon's servants. [4] Some of the sons of Judah and some of the sons of Benjamin lived in Jerusalem. From the sons of Judah: Athaiah the son of Uzziah, the son of Zechariah, the son of Amariah, the son of Shephatiah, the son of Mahalalel, of the sons of Perez; [5] and Maaseiah the son of Baruch, the son of Col-hozeh, the son of Hazaiah, the son of Adaiah, the son of Joiarib, the son of Zechariah, the son of the Shilonite. [6] All the sons of Perez who lived in Jerusalem were 468 able men.

[Leaders in Jerusalem] [7]   Now these are the sons of Benjamin: Sallu the son of Meshullam, the son of Joed, the son of Pedaiah, the son of Kolaiah, the son of Maaseiah, the son of Ithiel, the son of Jeshaiah; [8] and after him Gabbai *and* Sallai, 928. [9] Joel the son of Zichri was their overseer, and Judah the son of Hassenuah was second [1]in command of the city.

[Leaders in Jerusalem] [10]   From the priests: Jedaiah the son of Joiarib, Jachin, [11] Seraiah the son of Hilkiah, the son of Meshullam, the son of Zadok, the son of Meraioth, the son of Ahitub, the leader of the house of God, [12] and their [1]kinsmen who performed the work of the [2]temple, 822; and Adaiah the son of Jeroham, the son of Pelaliah, the son of Amzi, the son of Zechariah, the son of Pashhur, the son of Malchijah, [13] and his kinsmen, heads of fathers' *households,* 242; and Amashsai the son of Azarel, the son of Ahzai, the son of Meshillemoth, the son of Immer, [14] and their brothers, valiant warriors, 128. And their overseer was Zabdiel, the son of [1]Haggedolim.

[Leaders in Jerusalem] [15]   Now from the Levites: Shemaiah the son of Hasshub, the son of Azrikam, the son of Hashabiah, the son of Bunni; [16] and Shabbethai and Jozabad, from the [1]leaders of the Levites, who were [2]in charge of *a*the outside work of the house of God; [17] and Mattaniah the son of Mica, the son of [1]Zabdi, the son of Asaph, who was the [2]leader in beginning the thanksgiving at prayer, and Bakbukiah, the second among his brethren; and [3]Abda the son of [4]Shammua, the son of Galal, the son of Jeduthun. **18** All the Levites in *a*the holy city *were* 284.

[Leaders in Jerusalem] [19] Also the gatekeepers, Akkub, Talmon and their brethren who kept watch at the gates, *were* 172. **20** The rest of Israel, of the priests *and* of the Levites, *were* in all the cities of Judah, each *a*on his own inheritance. **21** But *a*the temple servants were living in Ophel, and Ziha and Gishpa were [1]in charge of the temple servants.

[Leaders in Jerusalem] [22] Now *a*the overseer of the Levites in Jerusalem was Uzzi the son of Bani, the son of Hashabiah, the son of Mattaniah, the son of Mica, from the sons of Asaph, who were the singers for the [1]service of the house of God. **23** *a*For *there was* a commandment from the king concerning them and a firm regulation for the song leaders *b*day by day. **24** Pethahiah the son of Meshezabel, of the sons *a*of Zerah the son of Judah, was the *b*king's [1]representative in all matters concerning the people.

[Leaders in the villages] [25] Now as for the villages with their fields, some of the sons of Judah lived in *a*Kiriath-arba and its [1]towns, in *b*Dibon and its [1]towns, and in Jekabzeel and its villages, **26** and in Jeshua, in Moladah and Beth-pelet, **27** and in Hazar-shual, in Beersheba and its towns, **28** and in Ziklag, in Meconah and in its towns, **29** and in En-rimmon, in Zorah and in Jarmuth, **30** Zanoah, Adullam, and their villages, Lachish and its fields, Azekah and its towns. So they encamped from Beersheba as far as the valley of Hinnom. **31** The sons of Benjamin also *lived* from Geba *onward,* at Michmash and Aija, at Bethel and its towns, **32** at Anathoth, Nob, Ananiah, **33** Hazor, Ramah, Gittaim, **34** Hadid, Zeboim, Neballat, **35** Lod and Ono, the valley of craftsmen. **36** From the Levites, *some* divisions in Judah belonged to Benjamin.

Questioning the Passage

1. Why were only a tenth of the people allowed into the city? (v. 1)

   Jerusalem was in ruins and had to have houses rebuilt. If Nehemiah allowed everyone who wanted to return to the city, the rebuilding would have failed. There was not enough food or shelter for the once large population of the city. As the city rebuilt, more people could live in Jerusalem.

2. Why were people blessed for living in Jerusalem? (v. 2)

   This verse is implying that not all the people selected in the tithe returned to the city. With the city destroyed, it would have been a problematic existance. Cities in Nehemiah's day were crowded and overpopolated. Therefore, the memory of what Jerusalem was like must have been told to the people. Many persons elected to live in small towns. In addition, the people were farmers. It is difficult to run a farm in the city.

Thoughts

In this chapter, Nehemiah identifies the leaders of Jerusalem and Judah.

Chapter Twelve

Language

New American Standard 1995	Hebrew
Neh. 12:1 Now these are ^athe priests and the Levites who came up with Zerubbabel the son of Shealtiel, and Jeshua: Seraiah, Jeremiah, Ezra, ² Amariah, Malluch, Hattush, ³ Shecaniah, Rehum, Meremoth, ⁴ Iddo, Ginnethoi, Abijah, ⁵ Mijamin, Maadiah, Bilgah, ⁶ Shemaiah and Joiarib, Jedaiah, ⁷ Sallu, Amok, Hilkiah and Jedaiah. These were the heads of the priests and their ¹kinsmen in the days of Jeshua. **Neh. 12:8** The Levites *were* Jeshua, Binnui, Kadmiel, Sherebiah, Judah, *and* Mattaniah *who was* ¹in charge of the songs of thanksgiving, he and his brothers. ⁹ Also Bakbukiah and Unni, their brothers, stood opposite them ^ain *their* service divisions. ¹⁰ Jeshua ¹became the father of Joiakim, and Joiakim ¹became the father of Eliashib, and Eliashib ¹became the father of Joiada, ¹¹ and Joiada became the father of Jonathan, and Jonathan became the father of Jaddua. **Neh. 12:12** Now in the days of Joiakim, the priests, the heads of fathers' *households* were: of Seraiah, Meraiah; of Jeremiah, Hananiah; ¹³ of Ezra, Meshullam; of Amariah, Jehohanan; ¹⁴ of ¹Malluchi, Jonathan; of Shebaniah, Joseph; ¹⁵ of Harim, Adna; of Meraioth, Helkai; ¹⁶ of Iddo, Zechariah; of Ginnethon,	וְאֵ֙לֶּה֙ הַכֹּהֲנִ֣ים וְהַלְוִיִּ֔ם Neh. 12:1 אֲשֶׁ֥ר עָל֖וּ עִם־זְרֻבָּבֶ֣ל בֶּן־ שְׁאַלְתִּיאֵ֖ל וְיֵשׁ֑וּעַ שְׂרָיָ֥ה יִרְמְיָ֖ה עֶזְרָֽא ׃ ² אֲמַרְיָ֥ה מַלּ֖וּךְ חַטּֽוּשׁ ׃ ³ שְׁכַנְיָ֥ה רְחֻ֖ם מְרֵמֹֽת ׃ ⁴ עִדּ֥וֹא גִנְּתֽוֹי אֲבִיָּֽה ׃ ⁵ מִיָּמִ֥ין מַֽעַדְיָ֖ה בִּלְגָּֽה ׃ ⁶ שְׁמַֽעְיָ֥ה וְיוֹיָרִ֖יב יְדַֽעְיָֽה ׃ ⁷ סַלּ֛וּ עָמ֖וֹק חִלְקִיָּ֣ה יְדַֽעְיָ֑ה אֵ֥לֶּה רָאשֵׁ֧י הַכֹּהֲנִ֛ים וַאֲחֵיהֶ֖ם בִּימֵ֥י יֵשֽׁוּעַ ׃ פ ⁸ וְהַלְוִיִּ֗ם יֵשׁ֧וּעַ בִּנּ֛וּי קַדְמִיאֵ֥ל שֵׁרֵֽבְיָ֖ה יְהוּדָ֑ה מַתַּנְיָ֛ה עַל־הֻיְדֹ֖ות ה֥וּא וְאֶחָֽיו ׃ ⁹ וּבַקְבֻּקְיָ֧ה וְעֻנּ֛וֹ [וְ][עֻנִּ֥י] אֲחֵיהֶ֖ם לְנֶגְדָּ֑ם לְמִשְׁמָרֽוֹת ׃ ¹⁰ וְיֵשׁ֖וּעַ הוֹלִ֣יד אֶת־ יֽוֹיָקִ֑ים וְיֽוֹיָקִים֙ הוֹלִ֣יד אֶת־אֶלְיָשִׁ֔יב וְאֶלְיָשִׁ֖יב אֶת־יוֹיָדָֽע ׃ ¹¹ וְיוֹיָדָ֗ע הוֹלִ֤יד אֶת־יֽוֹנָתָ֔ן וְיֽוֹנָתָ֖ן הוֹלִ֥יד אֶת־יַדּֽוּעַ ׃ ¹² וּבִימֵי֙ יֽוֹיָקִ֔ים הָי֣וּ כֹהֲנִ֔ים רָאשֵׁ֖י הָֽאָב֑וֹת לִשְׂרָיָ֣ה מְרָיָ֔ה לְיִרְמְיָ֖ה חֲנַנְיָֽה ׃ ¹³ לְעֶזְרָ֣א מְשֻׁלָּ֔ם לַאֲמַרְיָ֖ה יְהֽוֹחָנָֽן ׃ ¹⁴ לִמְלוּכִי֙ [לִ][מְלִיכוּ֙] יֽוֹנָתָ֔ן לִשְׁבַנְיָ֖ה יוֹסֵֽף ׃ ¹⁵ לְחָרִ֣ם עַדְנָ֔א

Meshullam; **17** of Abijah, Zichri; of Miniamin, of Moadiah, Piltai; **18** of Bilgah, Shammua; of Shemaiah, Jehonathan; **19** of Joiarib, Mattenai; of Jedaiah, Uzzi; **20** of Sallai, Kallai; of Amok, Eber; **21** of Hilkiah, Hashabiah; of Jedaiah, Nethanel.

Neh. 12:22 As for the Levites, the heads of fathers' *households* were registered in the days of Eliashib, Joiada, and Johanan and Jaddua; so *were* the priests in the reign of Darius the Persian. **23** The sons of Levi, the heads of fathers' *households,* were registered in the Book of the Chronicles up to the days of Johanan the son of Eliashib. **24** The heads of the Levites *were* Hashabiah, Sherebiah and Jeshua the son of Kadmiel, with their brothers opposite them, *a*to praise *and* give thanks, *1*as prescribed by David the man of God, *b*division corresponding to division. **25** Mattaniah, Bakbukiah, Obadiah, Meshullam, Talmon *and* Akkub *were* gatekeepers keeping watch at *a*the storehouses of the gates. **26** These *served* in the days of Joiakim the son of Jeshua, the son of Jozadak, and in the days of *a*Nehemiah the governor and of Ezra the priest *and* scribe.

Neh. 12:27 Now at the dedication of the wall of Jerusalem they sought out the Levites from all their places, to bring them to Jerusalem so that they might celebrate the dedication with gladness, with hymns of thanksgiving and with songs *a*to *the accompaniment* of cymbals, harps and lyres. **28** So the sons of the singers were assembled from the district around Jerusalem, and from *a*the villages of the Netophathites, **29** from Beth-gilgal

לְמָרֵיוֹת חֶלְקָי ׃ ¹⁶ לַעֲדָיָא
[לַ][עִדּוֹא] זְכַרְיָה לִגִנְּתוֹן מְשֻׁלָּם ׃
¹⁷ לַאֲבִיָּה זִכְרִי לְמִנְיָמִין לְמוֹעַדְיָה
פַּלְטָי ׃ ¹⁸ לְבִלְגָּה שַׁמּוּעַ לִשְׁמַעְיָה
יְהוֹנָתָן ׃ ¹⁹ וּלְיוֹיָרִיב מַתְּנַי לִידַעְיָה
עֻזִּי ׃ ²⁰ לְסַלַּי קַלָּי לְעָמוֹק עֵבֶר ׃ ²¹
לְחִלְקִיָּה חֲשַׁבְיָה לִידַעְיָה נְתַנְאֵל ׃
²² הַלְוִיִּם בִּימֵי אֶלְיָשִׁיב יוֹיָדָע
וְיוֹחָנָן וְיַדּוּעַ כְּתוּבִים רָאשֵׁי אָבוֹת
וְהַכֹּהֲנִים עַל־מַלְכוּת דָּרְיָוֶשׁ
הַפָּרְסִי ׃ פ ²³ בְּנֵי לֵוִי רָאשֵׁי הָאָבוֹת
כְּתוּבִים עַל־סֵפֶר דִּבְרֵי הַיָּמִים
וְעַד־יְמֵי יוֹחָנָן בֶּן־אֶלְיָשִׁיב ׃ ²⁴
וְרָאשֵׁי הַלְוִיִּם חֲשַׁבְיָה שֵׁרֵבְיָה
וְיֵשׁוּעַ בֶּן־קַדְמִיאֵל וַאֲחֵיהֶם
לְנֶגְדָּם לְהַלֵּל לְהוֹדוֹת בְּמִצְוַת
דָּוִיד אִישׁ־הָאֱלֹהִים מִשְׁמָר לְעֻמַּת
מִשְׁמָר ׃ ²⁵ מַתַּנְיָה וּבַקְבֻּקְיָה
עֹבַדְיָה מְשֻׁלָּם טַלְמוֹן עַקּוּב
שֹׁמְרִים שׁוֹעֲרִים מִשְׁמָר בַּאֲסֻפֵּי
הַשְּׁעָרִים ׃ ²⁶ אֵלֶּה בִּימֵי יוֹיָקִים בֶּן־
יֵשׁוּעַ בֶּן־יוֹצָדָק וּבִימֵי נְחֶמְיָה
הַפֶּחָה וְעֶזְרָא הַכֹּהֵן הַסּוֹפֵר ׃ פ ²⁷
וּבַחֲנֻכַּת חוֹמַת יְרוּשָׁלַ͏ִם בִּקְשׁוּ אֶת־
הַלְוִיִּם מִכָּל־מְקוֹמֹתָם לַהֲבִיאָם
לִירוּשָׁלָ͏ִם לַעֲשֹׂת חֲנֻכָּה וְשִׂמְחָה
וּבְתוֹדוֹת וּבְשִׁיר מְצִלְתַּיִם נְבָלִים
וּבְכִנֹּרוֹת ׃ ²⁸ וַיֵּאָסְפוּ בְּנֵי

and from *their* fields in Geba and Azmaveth, for the singers had built themselves villages around Jerusalem. **30** The priests and the Levites ͣpurified themselves; they also purified the people, the gates and the wall.

Neh. 12:31 Then I had the leaders of Judah come up on top of the wall, and I appointed two great ¹choirs, ²ͣthe first proceeding to the right on top of the wall toward ͣthe Refuse Gate. **32** Hoshaiah and half of the leaders of Judah followed them, **33** with Azariah, Ezra, Meshullam, **34** Judah, Benjamin, Shemaiah, Jeremiah, **35** and some of the sons of the priests with trumpets; *and* Zechariah the son of Jonathan, the son of Shemaiah, the son of Mattaniah, the son of Micaiah, the son of Zaccur, the son of Asaph, **36** and his ¹kinsmen, Shemaiah, Azarel, Milalai, Gilalai, Maai, Nethanel, Judah *and* Hanani, ͣwith the musical instruments of David the man of God. And Ezra the scribe went before them. **37** At ͣthe Fountain Gate they went directly up ͣthe steps of the city of David by the stairway of the wall above the house of David to ͨthe Water Gate on the east.

Neh. 12:38 ͣThe second ¹choir proceeded to the ²left, while I followed them with half of the people on the wall, ͣabove the Tower of Furnaces, to ͨthe Broad Wall, **39** and above ͣthe Gate of Ephraim, by ͣthe Old Gate, by the ͨFish Gate, ͩthe Tower of Hananel and the Tower of the Hundred, as far as the Sheep Gate; and they stopped at ͤthe Gate of the Guard. **40** Then the two choirs took their stand in the house of God. So did I

הַמְשֹׁרְרִים וּמִן־הַכִּכָּר סְבִיבוֹת

‏29 יְרוּשָׁלַם וּמִן־חַצְרֵי נְטֹפָתִי ׃

וּמִבֵּית הַגִּלְגָּל וּמִשְּׂדוֹת גֶּבַע

וְעַזְמָוֶת כִּי חֲצֵרִים בָּנוּ לָהֶם

‏30 הַמְשֹׁרְרִים סְבִיבוֹת יְרוּשָׁלָ͏ִם ׃

וַיִּטַּהֲרוּ הַכֹּהֲנִים וְהַלְוִיִּם וַיְטַהֲרוּ

אֶת־הָעָם וְאֶת־הַשְּׁעָרִים וְאֶת־

‏31 הַחוֹמָה ׃ וָאַעֲלֶה אֶת־שָׂרֵי יְהוּדָה

מֵעַל לַחוֹמָה וָאַעֲמִידָה שְׁתֵּי תוֹדֹת

גְּדוֹלֹת וְתַהֲלֻכֹת לַיָּמִין מֵעַל

‏32 לַחוֹמָה לְשַׁעַר הָאַשְׁפֹּת ׃ וַיֵּלֶךְ

אַחֲרֵיהֶם הוֹשַׁעְיָה וַחֲצִי שָׂרֵי

‏33 יְהוּדָה ׃ וַעֲזַרְיָה עֶזְרָא וּמְשֻׁלָּם ׃

‏34 יְהוּדָה וּבִנְיָמִן וּשְׁמַעְיָה וְיִרְמְיָה ׃

‏35 ס וּמִבְּנֵי הַכֹּהֲנִים בַּחֲצֹצְרוֹת

זְכַרְיָה בֶן־יוֹנָתָן בֶּן־שְׁמַעְיָה בֶּן־

מַתַּנְיָה בֶּן־מִיכָיָה בֶּן־זַכּוּר בֶּן־

‏36 אָסָף ׃ וְאֶחָיו שְׁמַעְיָה וַעֲזַרְאֵל

מִלֲלַי גִּלֲלַי מָעַי נְתַנְאֵל וִיהוּדָה

חֲנָנִי בִּכְלֵי־שִׁיר דָּוִיד אִישׁ

הָאֱלֹהִים וְעֶזְרָא הַסּוֹפֵר לִפְנֵיהֶם ׃

‏37 וְעַל שַׁעַר הָעַיִן וְנֶגְדָּם עָלוּ עַל־

מַעֲלוֹת עִיר דָּוִיד בַּמַּעֲלֶה לַחוֹמָה

מֵעַל לְבֵית דָּוִיד וְעַד שַׁעַר הַמַּיִם

‏38 מִזְרָח ׃ וְהַתּוֹדָה הַשֵּׁנִית הַהוֹלֶכֶת

לְמוֹאל וַאֲנִי אַחֲרֶיהָ וַחֲצִי הָעָם

מֵעַל לְהַחוֹמָה מֵעַל לְמִגְדַּל

‏39 הַתַּנּוּרִים וְעַד הַחוֹמָה הָרְחָבָה ׃

and half of the officials with me; **41** and the priests, Eliakim, Maaseiah, Miniamin, Micaiah, Elioenai, Zechariah and Hananiah, with the trumpets; **42** and Maaseiah, Shemaiah, Eleazar, Uzzi, Jehohanan, Malchijah, Elam and Ezer. And the singers [1]sang, with Jezrahiah *their* leader, **43** and on that day they offered great sacrifices and rejoiced because [a]God had given them great joy, even the women and children rejoiced, so that the joy of Jerusalem was heard from afar.

Neh. 12:44 On that day [a]men were also appointed over the chambers for the stores, the contributions, the first fruits and the tithes, to gather into them from the fields of the cities the portions required by the law for the priests and Levites; for Judah rejoiced over the priests and Levites who [1]served. **45** For they performed the [1]worship of their God and the service of purification, together with the singers and the gatekeepers [a]in accordance with the command of David *and* of his son Solomon. **46** For in the days of David and [a]Asaph, in ancient times, *there were* [1b]leaders of the singers, songs of praise and hymns of thanksgiving to God. **47** So all Israel in the days of Zerubbabel and Nehemiah gave the portions due the singers and the gatekeepers [a]as each day required, and [b]set apart the consecrated *portion* for the Levites, and the Levites set apart the consecrated *portion* for the sons of Aaron.

וּמֵעַל לְשַׁעַר־אֶפְרַיִם וְעַל־שַׁעַר הַיְשָׁנָה וְעַל־שַׁעַר הַדָּגִים וּמִגְדַּל חֲנַנְאֵל וּמִגְדַּל הַמֵּאָה וְעַד שַׁעַר הַצֹּאן וְעָמְדוּ בְּשַׁעַר הַמַּטָּרָה׃ 40

וַתַּעֲמֹדְנָה שְׁתֵּי הַתּוֹדֹת בְּבֵית הָאֱלֹהִים וַאֲנִי וַחֲצִי הַסְּגָנִים עִמִּי׃

41 וְהַכֹּהֲנִים אֶלְיָקִים מַעֲשֵׂיָה מִנְיָמִין מִיכָיָה אֶלְיוֹעֵינַי זְכַרְיָה חֲנַנְיָה בַּחֲצֹצְרוֹת׃ 42 וּמַעֲשֵׂיָה וּשְׁמַעְיָה וְאֶלְעָזָר וְעֻזִּי וִיהוֹחָנָן וּמַלְכִּיָּה וְעֵילָם וָעָזֶר וַיַּשְׁמִיעוּ הַמְשֹׁרְרִים וְיִזְרַחְיָה הַפָּקִיד׃ 43 וַיִּזְבְּחוּ בַיּוֹם־הַהוּא זְבָחִים גְּדוֹלִים וַיִּשְׂמָחוּ כִּי הָאֱלֹהִים שִׂמְּחָם שִׂמְחָה גְדוֹלָה וְגַם הַנָּשִׁים וְהַיְלָדִים שָׂמֵחוּ וַתִּשָּׁמַע שִׂמְחַת יְרוּשָׁלַ͏ִם מֵרָחוֹק׃ 44 וַיִּפָּקְדוּ בַיּוֹם הַהוּא אֲנָשִׁים עַל־הַנְּשָׁכוֹת לָאוֹצָרוֹת לַתְּרוּמוֹת לָרֵאשִׁית וְלַמַּעַשְׂרוֹת לִכְנוֹס בָּהֶם לִשְׂדֵי הֶעָרִים מְנָאוֹת הַתּוֹרָה לַכֹּהֲנִים וְלַלְוִיִּם כִּי שִׂמְחַת יְהוּדָה עַל־הַכֹּהֲנִים וְעַל־הַלְוִיִּם הָעֹמְדִים׃ 45 וַיִּשְׁמְרוּ מִשְׁמֶרֶת אֱלֹהֵיהֶם וּמִשְׁמֶרֶת הַטָּהֳרָה וְהַמְשֹׁרְרִים וְהַשֹּׁעֲרִים כְּמִצְוַת דָּוִיד שְׁלֹמֹה בְנוֹ׃ 46 כִּי־בִימֵי דָוִיד וְאָסָף מִקֶּדֶם רֹאשׁ [רָאשֵׁי] הַמְשֹׁרְרִים וְשִׁיר־תְּהִלָּה וְהֹדוֹת לֵאלֹהִים׃ 47 וְכָל־

<table>
<tr>
<td></td>
<td dir="rtl">

יִשְׂרָאֵל בִּימֵי זְרֻבָּבֶל וּבִימֵי נְחֶמְיָה
נְתֻנִים מְנָיוֹת הַמְשֹׁרְרִים וְהַשֹּׁעֲרִים
דְּבַר־יוֹם בְּיוֹמוֹ וּמַקְדִּשִׁים לַלְוִיִּם
וְהַלְוִיִּם מַקְדִּשִׁים לִבְנֵי אַהֲרֹן׃ פ

</td>
</tr>
</table>

References

Nehemiah 12:1 [a]Ezra 2:1; 7:7	**Nehemiah 12:37** [a]Neh 2:14 [b]Neh 3:15 [c]Neh 3:26
Nehemiah 12:7 [1]Lit *brothers*	
	Nehemiah 12:38 [1]Lit *thanksgiving choir* [2]Lit *front* [a]Neh 12:31 [b]Neh 3:11 [c]Neh 3:8
Nehemiah 12:8 [1]Lit *over*	
Nehemiah 12:9 [a]Neh 12:24	
Nehemiah 12:10 [1]Lit *begot,* and so in vv 11, 12	**Nehemiah 12:39** [a]Neh 8:16 [b]Neh 3:6 [c]Neh 3:3 [d]Neh 3:1 [e]Neh 3:25
Nehemiah 12:14 [1]In Neh 12:2, *Malluch*	
Nehemiah 12:24 [1]Lit *in the commandment of* [a]Neh 11:17 [b]Neh 12:9	**Nehemiah 12:42** [1]Lit *caused their voices to be heard*
	Nehemiah 12:43 [a]Ps 9:2; 92:4
Nehemiah 12:25 [a]1 Chr 26:15	
	Nehemiah 12:44 [1]Lit *stood* [a]Neh 13:4, 5, 12, 13
Nehemiah 12:26 [a]Neh 8:9	
Nehemiah 12:27 [a]1 Chr 15:16, 28	**Nehemiah 12:45** [1]Lit *service* [a]1 Chr 25:1
Nehemiah 12:28 [a]1 Chr 9:16	**Nehemiah 12:46** [1]Lit *heads* [a]2 Chr 29:30 [b]1 Chr 9:33
Nehemiah 12:30 [a]Neh 13:22, 30	
Nehemiah 12:31	**Nehemiah 12:47**

<table>
<tr><td>

¹Lit *thanksgiving choirs*
²Heb *and processions to the right*
ᵃNeh 12:38
ᵇNeh 2:13

Nehemiah 12:36
¹Lit *brothers*
ᵃNeh 12:24

</td><td>

ᵃNeh 11:23
ᵇNum 18:21

</td></tr>
</table>

Process of Discovery

Linguistics Section

Linguistic Structure

[Names of Priests] [1]   Now these are *the priests and the Levites who came up with Zerubbabel the son of Shealtiel, and Jeshua: Seraiah, Jeremiah, Ezra, [2] Amariah, Malluch, Hattush, [3] Shecaniah, Rehum, Meremoth, [4] Iddo, Ginnethoi, Abijah, [5] Mijamin, Maadiah, Bilgah, [6] Shemaiah and Joiarib, Jedaiah, [7] Sallu, Amok, Hilkiah and Jedaiah. These were the heads of the priests and their [1]kinsmen in the days of Jeshua.

[Names of the Levites] 7   The Levites *were* Jeshua, Binnui, Kadmiel, Sherebiah, Judah, *and* Mattaniah *who was* [1]in charge of the songs of thanksgiving, he and his brothers. [9] Also Bakbukiah and Unni, their brothers, stood opposite them *a*in *their* service divisions. [10] Jeshua [1]became the father of Joiakim, and Joiakim [1]became the father of Eliashib, and Eliashib [1]became the father of Joiada, [11] and Joiada became the father of Jonathan, and Jonathan became the father of Jaddua.

[Joiakim's days] [12]   Now in the days of Joiakim, the priests, the heads of fathers' *households* were: of Seraiah, Meraiah; of Jeremiah, Hananiah; [13] of Ezra, Meshullam; of Amariah, Jehohanan; [14] of [1]Malluchi, Jonathan; of Shebaniah, Joseph; [15] of Harim, Adna; of Meraioth, Helkai; [16] of Iddo, Zechariah; of Ginnethon, Meshullam; [17] of Abijah, Zichri; of Miniamin, of Moadiah, Piltai; [18] of Bilgah, Shammua; of Shemaiah, Jehonathan; [19] of Joiarib, Mattenai; of Jedaiah, Uzzi; [20] of Sallai, Kallai; of Amok, Eber; [21] of Hilkiah, Hashabiah; of Jedaiah, Nethanel.

[Levites] [22] As for the Levites, the heads of fathers' *households* were registered in the days of Eliashib, Joiada, and Johanan and Jaddua; so *were* the priests in the reign of Darius the Persian. [23] The sons of Levi, the heads of fathers' *households,* were registered in the Book of the Chronicles up to the days of Johanan the son of Eliashib. [24] The heads of the Levites *were* Hashabiah, Sherebiah and Jeshua the son of Kadmiel, with their brothers opposite them, *a*to praise *and* give thanks, [1]as prescribed by David the man of God, *b*division corresponding to division. [25] Mattaniah, Bakbukiah, Obadiah, Meshullam, Talmon *and* Akkub *were* gatekeepers keeping watch at *a*the storehouses of the gates. [26] These *served* in the days of Joiakim the son of Jeshua, the son of Jozadak, and in the days of *a*Nehemiah the governor and of Ezra the priest *and* scribe.

[For the wall dedication] [27] Now at the dedication of the wall of Jerusalem they sought out the Levites from all their places, to bring them to Jerusalem so that they might celebrate the dedication with gladness, with hymns of thanksgiving and with songs *to the accompaniment* of cymbals, harps and lyres. **28** So the sons of the singers were assembled from the district around Jerusalem, and from *the villages of the Netophathites, **29** from Beth-gilgal and from *their* fields in Geba and Azmaveth, for the singers had built themselves villages around Jerusalem. **30** The priests and the Levites *purified themselves; they also purified the people, the gates and the wall.

[The leaders of Judah] **31** Then I had the leaders of Judah come up on top of the wall, and I appointed two great [1]choirs, [2a]the first proceeding to the right on top of the wall toward *the Refuse Gate. **32** Hoshaiah and half of the leaders of Judah followed them, **33** with Azariah, Ezra, Meshullam, **34** Judah, Benjamin, Shemaiah, Jeremiah, **35** and some of the sons of the priests with trumpets; *and* Zechariah the son of Jonathan, the son of Shemaiah, the son of Mattaniah, the son of Micaiah, the son of Zaccur, the son of Asaph, **36** and his [1]kinsmen, Shemaiah, Azarel, Milalai, Gilalai, Maai, Nethanel, Judah *and* Hanani, *with the musical instruments of David the man of God. And Ezra the scribe went before them. **37** At *the Fountain Gate they went directly up *the steps of the city of David by the stairway of the wall above the house of David to *the Water Gate on the east.

[The choir] **38** *The second [1]choir proceeded to the [2]left, while I followed them with half of the people on the wall, *above the Tower of Furnaces, to *the Broad Wall, **39** and above *the Gate of Ephraim, by *the Old Gate, by the *Fish Gate, *the Tower of Hananel and the Tower of the Hundred, as far as the Sheep Gate; and they stopped at *the Gate of the Guard. **40** Then the two choirs took their stand in the house of God. So did I and half of the officials with me; **41** and the priests, Eliakim, Maaseiah, Miniamin, Micaiah, Elioenai, Zechariah and Hananiah, with the trumpets; **42** and Maaseiah, Shemaiah, Eleazar, Uzzi, Jehohanan, Malchijah, Elam and Ezer. And the singers [1]sang, with Jezrahiah *their* leader, **43** and on that day they offered great sacrifices and rejoiced because *God had given them great joy, even the women and children rejoiced, so that the joy of Jerusalem was heard from afar.

[Chambers for the stores] On that day *men were also appointed over the chambers for the stores, the contributions, the first fruits and the tithes, to gather into them from the fields of the cities the portions required by the law for the priests and Levites; for Judah rejoiced over the priests and Levites who [1]served. **45** For they performed the [1]worship of their God and the service of purification, together with the singers and the gatekeepers *in accordance with the command of David *and* of his son Solomon. **46** For in the days of David and *Asaph, in ancient times, *there were* [1b]leaders of the singers, songs of praise and hymns of thanksgiving to God. **47** So all Israel in the days of Zerubbabel and Nehemiah gave the portions due the singers and the gatekeepers *as each day required, and *set apart the consecrated *portion* for the Levites, and the Levites set apart the consecrated *portion* for the sons of Aaron.

135

Thoughts

The completion of the walls of Jerusalem was an historical milestone. Nehemiah's task was to go to Jerusalem and see that this happened. He fought against a lot of people who wanted to stop him. With the LORD Nehemiah and the people were able to build and dedicate the walls.

Chapter Thirteen

Language

New American Standard 1995	Hebrew
Neh. 13:1 On that day ^athey read aloud from the book of Moses in the hearing of the people; and there was found written in it that ^bno Ammonite or Moabite should ever enter the assembly of God, **2** because they did not meet the sons of Israel with bread and water, but ^ahired Balaam against them to curse them. However, ^bour God turned the curse into a blessing. **3** So when they heard the law, ^athey excluded ^ball foreigners from Israel. **Neh. 13:4** Now prior to this, Eliashib the priest, ^awho was appointed over the chambers of the house of our God, being ¹related to ^bTobiah, **5** had prepared a large ¹room for him, where formerly they put the grain offerings, the frankincense, the utensils and the tithes of grain, wine and oil ^aprescribed for the Levites, the singers and the gatekeepers, and the ²contributions for the priests. **6** But during all this *time* I was not in Jerusalem, for in ^athe thirty-second year of ^bArtaxerxes king of Babylon I had gone to the king. After some time, however, I asked leave from the king, **7** and I came to Jerusalem and ¹learned about the evil that Eliashib had done for Tobiah, ^aby preparing a ²room for him in the courts of the house of God. **8** It was very displeasing to me, so I ^athrew all of Tobiah's household goods out of the room. **9** Then I gave an order and ^athey cleansed the rooms; and I returned there the utensils of the house of	בַּיּוֹם הַהוּא נִקְרָא בְּסֵפֶר Neh. 13:1 מֹשֶׁה בְּאָזְנֵי הָעָם וְנִמְצָא כָּתוּב בּוֹ אֲשֶׁר לֹא־יָבוֹא עַמֹּנִי וּמֹאָבִי בִּקְהַל הָאֱלֹהִים עַד־עוֹלָם: 2 כִּי לֹא קִדְּמוּ אֶת־בְּנֵי יִשְׂרָאֵל בַּלֶּחֶם וּבַמָּיִם וַיִּשְׂכֹּר עָלָיו אֶת־בִּלְעָם לְקַלְלוֹ וַיַּהֲפֹךְ אֱלֹהֵינוּ הַקְּלָלָה לִבְרָכָה: 3 וַיְהִי כְּשָׁמְעָם אֶת־ הַתּוֹרָה וַיַּבְדִּילוּ כָל־עֵרֶב מִיִּשְׂרָאֵל: 4 וְלִפְנֵי מִזֶּה אֶלְיָשִׁיב הַכֹּהֵן נָתוּן בְּלִשְׁכַּת בֵּית־אֱלֹהֵינוּ קָרוֹב לְטוֹבִיָּה: 5 וַיַּעַשׂ לוֹ לִשְׁכָּה גְדוֹלָה וְשָׁם הָיוּ לְפָנִים נֹתְנִים אֶת־ הַמִּנְחָה הַלְּבוֹנָה וְהַכֵּלִים וּמַעְשַׂר הַדָּגָן הַתִּירוֹשׁ וְהַיִּצְהָר מִצְוַת הַלְוִיִּם וְהַמְשֹׁרְרִים וְהַשֹּׁעֲרִים וּתְרוּמַת הַכֹּהֲנִים: 6 וּבְכָל־זֶה לֹא הָיִיתִי בִּירוּשָׁלִָם כִּי בִּשְׁנַת שְׁלֹשִׁים וּשְׁתַּיִם לְאַרְתַּחְשַׁסְתְּא מֶלֶךְ־בָּבֶל בָּאתִי אֶל־הַמֶּלֶךְ וּלְקֵץ יָמִים נִשְׁאַלְתִּי מִן־הַמֶּלֶךְ: 7 וָאָבוֹא לִירוּשָׁלִָם וָאָבִינָה בָרָעָה אֲשֶׁר עָשָׂה אֶלְיָשִׁיב לְטוֹבִיָּה לַעֲשׂוֹת לוֹ נִשְׁכָּה בְּחַצְרֵי בֵּית הָאֱלֹהִים: 8 וַיֵּרַע לִי מְאֹד וָאַשְׁלִיכָה אֶת־כָּל־

God with the grain offerings and the frankincense.

Neh. 13:10 I also [1]discovered that [a]the portions of the Levites had not been given *them,* so that the Levites and the singers who performed the service had [2]gone away, [b]each to his own field. **11** So I [1a]reprimanded the officials and said, "[b]Why is the house of God forsaken?" Then I gathered them together and restored them to their posts. **12** All Judah then brought [a]the tithe of the grain, wine and oil into the storehouses. **13** In charge of the storehouses I appointed Shelemiah the priest, Zadok the scribe, and Pedaiah of the Levites, and in addition to them was Hanan the son of Zaccur, the son of Mattaniah; for [a]they were considered reliable, and it was [1]their task to distribute to their [2]kinsmen. **14** [a]Remember me for this, O my God, and do not blot out my loyal deeds which I have performed for the house of my God and its services.

Neh. 13:15 In those days I saw in Judah some who were treading wine presses [a]on the sabbath, and bringing in sacks of grain and loading *them* on donkeys, as well as wine, grapes, figs and all kinds of loads, [b]and they brought *them* into Jerusalem on the sabbath day. So ʾI admonished *them* on the day they sold food. **16** Also men of Tyre were living [1]there *who* imported fish and all kinds of merchandise, and sold *them* to the sons of Judah on the sabbath, even in Jerusalem. **17** Then ʾI [1]reprimanded the nobles of Judah and said to them, "What is this evil thing you are doing, [2]by profaning the sabbath day? **18** "Did not your fathers do the same, so

כְּלֵי בֵית־טוֹבִיָּה הֶחוּץ מִן

הַלִּשְׁכָּה : 9 וָאֹמְרָה וַיְטַהֲרוּ

הַלְּשָׁכוֹת וָאָשִׁיבָה שָּׁם כְּלֵי בֵית

הָאֱלֹהִים אֶת־הַמִּנְחָה וְהַלְּבוֹנָה : פ

10 וָאֵדְעָה כִּי־מְנָיוֹת הַלְוִיִּם לֹא

נִתָּנָה וַיִּבְרְחוּ אִישׁ־לְשָׂדֵהוּ הַלְוִיִּם

וְהַמְשֹׁרְרִים עֹשֵׂי הַמְּלָאכָה : 11

וָאָרִיבָה אֶת־הַסְּגָנִים וָאֹמְרָה

מַדּוּעַ נֶעֱזַב בֵּית־הָאֱלֹהִים

וָאֶקְבְּצֵם וָאַעֲמִדֵם עַל־עָמְדָם : 12

וְכָל־יְהוּדָה הֵבִיאוּ מַעְשַׂר הַדָּגָן

וְהַתִּירוֹשׁ וְהַיִּצְהָר לָאוֹצָרוֹת : 13

וָאוֹצְרָה עַל־אוֹצָרוֹת שֶׁלֶמְיָה

הַכֹּהֵן וְצָדוֹק הַסּוֹפֵר וּפְדָיָה מִן־

הַלְוִיִּם וְעַל־יָדָם חָנָן בֶּן־זַכּוּר בֶּן־

מַתַּנְיָה כִּי נֶאֱמָנִים נֶחְשָׁבוּ וַעֲלֵיהֶם

לַחֲלֹק לַאֲחֵיהֶם : פ 14 זָכְרָה־לִּי

אֱלֹהַי עַל־זֹאת וְאַל־תֶּמַח חֲסָדַי

אֲשֶׁר עָשִׂיתִי בְּבֵית אֱלֹהַי

וּבְמִשְׁמָרָיו : 15 בַּיָּמִים הָהֵמָּה

רָאִיתִי בִיהוּדָה דֹרְכִים־גִּתּוֹת

בַּשַּׁבָּת וּמְבִיאִים הָעֲרֵמוֹת וְעֹמְסִים

עַל־הַחֲמֹרִים וְאַף־יַיִן עֲנָבִים

וּתְאֵנִים וְכָל־מַשָּׂא וּמְבִיאִים

יְרוּשָׁלַם בְּיוֹם הַשַּׁבָּת וָאָעִיד בְּיוֹם

מִכְרָם צָיִד : 16 וְהַצֹּרִים יָשְׁבוּ בָהּ

מְבִיאִים דָּאג וְכָל־מֶכֶר וּמֹכְרִים

בַּשַּׁבָּת לִבְנֵי יְהוּדָה וּבִירוּשָׁלָם : 17

that our God brought on us and on this city all this trouble? Yet you are adding to the wrath on Israel by profaning the sabbath."

Neh. 13:19 *ª*It came about that just as it grew dark at the gates of Jerusalem before the sabbath, I commanded that the doors should be shut [1]and that they should not open them until after the sabbath. Then I stationed some of my servants at the gates *so that* no load would enter on the sabbath day. [20] Once or twice the traders and merchants of every kind of merchandise spent the night outside Jerusalem. [21] Then *ª*I [1]warned them and said to them, "Why do you spend the night in front of the wall? If you do so again, I will [2]use force against you." From that time on they did not come on the sabbath. [22] And I commanded the Levites that *ª*they should purify themselves and come as gatekeepers to sanctify the sabbath day. *For* this also *b*remember me, O my God, and have compassion on me according to the greatness of Your lovingkindness.

Neh. 13:23 In those days I also saw that the Jews had [1ª]married women from *b*Ashdod, *c*Ammon *and* Moab. [24] As for their children, half spoke in the language of Ashdod, and none of them was able to speak the language of Judah, but [1]the language of his own people. [25] So *ª*I contended with them and cursed them and *b*struck some of them and pulled out their hair, and *c*made them swear by God, "You shall not give your daughters to their sons, nor take of their daughters for your sons or for yourselves. [26] *"ª*Did not Solomon king of Israel sin regarding

וָאָרִיבָה אֶת חֹרֵי יְהוּדָה וָאֹמְרָה
לָהֶם מָה־הַדָּבָר הָרָע הַזֶּה אֲשֶׁר
אַתֶּם עֹשִׂים וּמְחַלְּלִים אֶת־יוֹם
הַשַּׁבָּת ׃ 18 הֲלוֹא כֹה עָשׂוּ אֲבֹתֵיכֶם
וַיָּבֵא אֱלֹהֵינוּ עָלֵינוּ אֵת כָּל־הָרָעָה
הַזֹּאת וְעַל הָעִיר הַזֹּאת וְאַתֶּם
מוֹסִיפִים חָרוֹן עַל־יִשְׂרָאֵל לְחַלֵּל
אֶת־הַשַּׁבָּת ׃ פ 19 וַיְהִי כַּאֲשֶׁר צָלֲלוּ
שַׁעֲרֵי יְרוּשָׁלַ͏ִם לִפְנֵי הַשַּׁבָּת
וָאֹמְרָה וַיִּסָּגְרוּ הַדְּלָתוֹת וָאֹמְרָה
אֲשֶׁר לֹא יִפְתָּחוּם עַד אַחַר הַשַּׁבָּת
וּמִנְּעָרַי הֶעֱמַדְתִּי עַל־הַשְּׁעָרִים
לֹא־יָבוֹא מַשָּׂא בְּיוֹם הַשַּׁבָּת ׃ 20
וַיָּלִינוּ הָרֹכְלִים וּמֹכְרֵי כָל־מִמְכָּר
מִחוּץ לִירוּשָׁלָ͏ִם פַּעַם וּשְׁתָּיִם ׃ 21
וָאָעִידָה בָהֶם וָאֹמְרָה אֲלֵיהֶם
מַדּוּעַ אַתֶּם לֵנִים נֶגֶד הַחוֹמָה אִם־
תִּשְׁנוּ יָד אֶשְׁלַח בָּכֶם מִן־הָעֵת
הַהִיא לֹא־בָאוּ בַּשַּׁבָּת ׃ ס 22
וָאֹמְרָה לַלְוִיִּם אֲשֶׁר יִהְיוּ מִטַּהֲרִים
וּבָאִים שֹׁמְרִים הַשְּׁעָרִים לְקַדֵּשׁ
אֶת־יוֹם הַשַּׁבָּת גַּם־זֹאת זָכְרָה־לִּי
אֱלֹהַי וְחוּסָה עָלַי כְּרֹב חַסְדֶּךָ ׃ פ
23 גַּם ׀ בַּיָּמִים הָהֵם רָאִיתִי אֶת־
הַיְּהוּדִים הֹשִׁיבוּ נָשִׁים אַשְׁדּוֹדִיּוֹת
[אַשְׁדֳּדִיּוֹת] עַמֳּנִיּוֹת [עַמֳּנִיּוֹת]
מוֹאֲבִיּוֹת ׃ 24 וּבְנֵיהֶם חֲצִי מְדַבֵּר
אַשְׁדּוֹדִית וְאֵינָם מַכִּירִים לְדַבֵּר

these things? [b]Yet among the many nations there was no king like him, and [c]he was loved by his God, and God made him king over all Israel; nevertheless the foreign women caused even him to sin. **27** [c1]Do we then hear about you that you have committed all this great evil [a]by acting unfaithfully against our God by [2]marrying foreign women?" **28** Even one of the sons of Joiada, the son of Eliashib the high priest, was a son-in-law of [a]Sanballat the Horonite, so I drove him away from me. **29** [a]Remember them, O my God, [1]because they have defiled the priesthood and the [b]covenant of the priesthood and the Levites.

Neh. 13:30 [a]Thus I purified them from everything foreign and appointed duties for the priests and the Levites, each in his task, **31** and I *arranged* [a]for the supply of wood at appointed times and for the first fruits. [b]Remember me, O my God, for good.

יְהוּדִ֔ית וְכִלְשֹׁ֖ן עַ֣ם וָעָ֑ם 25 : וָאָרִ֤יב עִמָּם֙ וָאֲקַֽלְלֵ֔ם וָאַכֶּ֥ה מֵהֶ֖ם אֲנָשִׁ֑ים וָֽאֶמְרְטֵ֑ם וָאַשְׁבִּיעֵ֣ם בֵּֽאלֹהִ֔ים אִם־תִּתְּנ֤וּ בְנֹֽתֵיכֶם֙ לִבְנֵיהֶ֔ם וְאִם־תִּשְׂאוּ֙ מִבְּנֹֽתֵיהֶ֔ם לִבְנֵיכֶ֖ם וְלָכֶֽם 26 : הֲל֣וֹא עַל־אֵ֣לֶּה חָטָֽא־שְׁלֹמֹ֣ה מֶ֣לֶךְ יִשְׂרָאֵ֗ל וּבַגּוֹיִ֤ם הָֽרַבִּים֙ לֹא־הָיָ֣ה מֶ֣לֶךְ כָּמֹ֔הוּ וְאָה֤וּב לֵֽאלֹהָיו֙ הָיָ֔ה וַיִּתְּנֵ֣הוּ אֱלֹהִ֔ים מֶ֖לֶךְ עַל־כָּל־יִשְׂרָאֵ֑ל גַּם־אוֹתֹ֣ו הֶחֱטִ֔יאוּ הַנָּשִׁ֖ים הַנָּכְרִיּֽוֹת : 27 וְלָכֶ֣ם הֲנִשְׁמַ֗ע לַעֲשֹׂת֙ אֵ֣ת כָּל־הָרָעָ֤ה הַגְּדוֹלָה֙ הַזֹּ֔את לִמְעֹ֖ל בֵּֽאלֹהֵ֑ינוּ לְהֹשִׁ֖יב נָשִׁ֥ים נָכְרִיּֽוֹת : 28 וּמִבְּנֵ֨י יֽוֹיָדָ֤ע בֶּן־אֶלְיָשִׁיב֙ הַכֹּהֵ֣ן הַגָּד֔וֹל חָתָ֖ן לְסַנְבַלַּ֣ט הַחֹרֹנִ֑י וָאַבְרִיחֵ֖הוּ מֵעָלָֽי : 29 זָכְרָ֥ה לָהֶ֖ם אֱלֹהָ֑י עַ֚ל גָּֽאֳלֵ֣י הַכְּהֻנָּ֔ה וּבְרִ֥ית הַכְּהֻנָּ֖ה וְהַלְוִיִּֽם : 30 וְטִֽהַרְתִּ֖ים מִכָּל־נֵכָ֑ר וָאַעֲמִ֧ידָה מִשְׁמָר֛וֹת לַכֹּהֲנִ֥ים וְלַלְוִיִּ֖ם אִ֥ישׁ בִּמְלַאכְתּֽוֹ : 31 וּלְקֻרְבַּ֧ן הָעֵצִ֛ים בְּעִתִּ֥ים מְזֻמָּנֹ֖ות וְלַבִּכּוּרִ֑ים זָכְרָה־לִּ֥י אֱלֹהַ֖י לְטוֹבָֽה :

References

Nehemiah 13:1
[a]Neh 9:3
[b]Deut 23:3-5; Neh 13:23

Nehemiah 13:2
[a]Num 22:3-11
[b]Deut 23:5

Nehemiah 13:3
[a]Neh 9:2; 10:28
[b]Ex 12:38

Nehemiah 13:4
[1]Lit *close to*
[a]Neh 12:44
[b]Neh 2:10; 6:1, 17, 18

Nehemiah 13:5
[1]Or *chamber*
[2]Lit *heave offerings*
[a]Num 18:21

Nehemiah 13:6
[a]Neh 5:14
[b]Ezra 6:22

Nehemiah 13:7
[1]Or *understood*
[2]Or *chamber,* and so in vv 8, 9
[a]Neh 13:5

Nehemiah 13:8
[a]John 2:13-16

Nehemiah 13:9
[a]2 Chr 29:5, 15, 16

Nehemiah 13:19
[1]Lit *and commanded*
[a]Lev 23:32

Nehemiah 13:21
[1]Lit *witnessed against*
[2]Lit *send a hand against*
[a]Neh 13:15

Nehemiah 13:22
[a]1 Chr 15:12; Neh 12:30
[b]Neh 13:14, 31

Nehemiah 13:23
[1]Lit *given dwelling to*
[a]Ex 34:11-16; Deut 7:1-5; Ezra 9:2; Neh 10:30
[b]Neh 4:7
[c]Ezra 9:1; Neh 13:1

Nehemiah 13:24
[1]Lit *according to the tongue of people and people*

Nehemiah 13:25
[a]Neh 13:11, 17
[b]Deut 25:2
[c]Neh 10:29, 30

Nehemiah 13:26
[a]1 Kin 11:1
[b]1 Kin 3:13; 2 Chr 1:12
[c]2 Sam 12:24, 25

Nehemiah 13:27
[1]Or *Is it reported*
[2]Lit *giving dwelling to*

Nehemiah 13:10
[1]Or *knew*
[2]Lit *fled*
[a]Deut 12:19; Neh 10:37
[b]Neh 12:28, 29

Nehemiah 13:11
[1]Or *contended with*
[a]Neh 13:17, 25
[b]Neh 10:39

Nehemiah 13:12
[a]Neh 10:37; 12:44; Mal 3:10

Nehemiah 13:13
[1]Lit *on them to*
[2]Lit *brothers*
[a]Neh 7:2

Nehemiah 13:14
[a]Neh 5:19; 13:22, 31

Nehemiah 13:15
[a]Ex 20:8; 34:21; Deut 5:12-14; Jer 17:22
[b]Neh 10:31; Jer 17:21
[c]Neh 9:29; 13:21

Nehemiah 13:16
[1]Lit *in it*

Nehemiah 13:17
[1]Or *contended with*
[2]Lit *and*
[a]Neh 13:11, 25

Nehemiah 13:18
[a]Ezra 9:13; Jer 17:21

[a]Ezra 10:2; Neh 13:23

Nehemiah 13:28
[a]Neh 2:10, 19; 4:1

Nehemiah 13:29
[1]Lit *for the defilings of*
[a]Neh 6:14
[b]Num 25:13

Nehemiah 13:30
[a]Neh 10:30

Nehemiah 13:31
[a]Neh 10:34
[b]Neh 13:14, 22

Process of Discovery

Linguistics Section

Linguistic Structure

[The Story of Balaam] [1] On that day [a]they read aloud from the book of Moses in the hearing of the people; and there was found written in it that [b]no Ammonite or Moabite should ever enter the assembly of God, [2] because they did not meet the sons of Israel with bread and water, but [a]hired Balaam against them to curse them. However, [b]our God turned the curse into a blessing. [3] So when they heard the law, [a]they excluded [b]all foreigners from Israel.

[Revolt] [4] Now prior to this, Eliashib the priest, [a]who was appointed over the chambers of the house of our God, being [1]related to [b]Tobiah, [5] had prepared a large [1]room for him, where formerly they put the grain offerings, the frankincense, the utensils and the tithes of grain, wine and oil [a]prescribed for the Levites, the singers and the gatekeepers, and the [2]contributions for the priests. [6] But during all this *time* I was not in Jerusalem, for in [a]the thirty-second year of [b]Artaxerxes king of Babylon I had gone to the king. After some time, however, I asked leave from the king, [7] and I came to Jerusalem and [1]learned about the evil that Eliashib had done for Tobiah, [a]by preparing a [2]room for him in the courts of the house of God. [8] It was very displeasing to me, so I [a]threw all of Tobiah's household goods out of the room. [9] Then I gave an order and [a]they cleansed the rooms; and I returned there the utensils of the house of God with the grain offerings and the frankincense.

[Tithes] [10] I also [1]discovered that [a]the portions of the Levites had not been given *them,* so that the Levites and the singers who performed the service had [2]gone away, [b]each to his own field. [11] So I [1a]reprimanded the officials and said, "[b]Why is the house of God forsaken?" Then I gathered them together and restored them to their posts. [12] All Judah then brought [a]the tithe of the grain, wine and oil into the storehouses. [13] In charge of the storehouses I appointed Shelemiah the priest, Zadok the scribe, and Pedaiah of the Levites, and in addition to them was Hanan the son of Zaccur, the son of Mattaniah; for [a]they were considered reliable, and it was [1]their task to distribute to their [2]kinsmen. [14] [a]Remember me for this, O my God, and do not blot out my loyal deeds which I have performed for the house of my God and its services.

[Sabbath] [15] In those days I saw in Judah some who were treading wine presses [a]on the sabbath, and bringing in sacks of grain and loading *them* on donkeys, as well as wine, grapes, figs and all kinds of loads, [b]and they brought *them* into Jerusalem on the sabbath day. So I admonished *them* on the day they sold food. [16] Also men of Tyre were living [1]there *who* imported fish and all kinds of merchandise, and sold *them* to the sons of Judah on the sabbath, even in Jerusalem. **17** Then *I* [1]reprimanded the nobles of Judah and said to them, "What is this evil thing you are doing, [2]by profaning the sabbath day? **18** "*a*Did not your fathers do the same, so that our God brought on us and on this city all this trouble? Yet you are adding to the wrath on Israel by profaning the sabbath."

[Sabbath] **19** *a*It came about that just as it grew dark at the gates of Jerusalem before the sabbath, I commanded that the doors should be shut [1]and that they should not open them until after the sabbath. Then I stationed some of my servants at the gates *so that* no load would enter on the sabbath day. **20** Once or twice the traders and merchants of every kind of merchandise spent the night outside Jerusalem. **21** Then *I* [1]warned them and said to them, "Why do you spend the night in front of the wall? If you do so again, I will [2]use force against you." From that time on they did not come on the sabbath. **22** And I commanded the Levites that *a*they should purify themselves and come as gatekeepers to sanctify the sabbath day. *For* this also *b*remember me, O my God, and have compassion on me according to the greatness of Your lovingkindness.

[Pagan marriage] **23** In those days I also saw that the Jews had [1]*a*married women from *b*Ashdod, *c*Ammon *and* Moab. **24** As for their children, half spoke in the language of Ashdod, and none of them was able to speak the language of Judah, but [1]the language of his own people. **25** So *a*I contended with them and cursed them and *b*struck some of them and pulled out their hair, and *c*made them swear by God, "You shall not give your daughters to their sons, nor take of their daughters for your sons or for yourselves. **26** "*a*Did not Solomon king of Israel sin regarding these things? *b*Yet among the many nations there was no king like him, and *c*he was loved by his God, and God made him king over all Israel; nevertheless the foreign women caused even him to sin. **27** "[1]Do we then hear about you that you have committed all this great evil *a*by acting unfaithfully against our God by [2]marrying foreign women?" **28** Even one of the sons of Joiada, the son of Eliashib the high priest, was a son-in-law of *a*Sanballat the Horonite, so I drove him away from me. **29** *a*Remember them, O my God, [1]because they have defiled the priesthood and the *b*covenant of the priesthood and the Levites.

[Purification] **30** *a*Thus I purified them from everything foreign and appointed duties for the priests and the Levites, each in his task, **31** and *I arranged* *a*for the supply of wood at appointed times and for the first fruits. *b*Remember me, O my God, for good.

Discussion

This chapter describes what happened to the people who returned to Jerusalem.

Questioning the Passage

1. Why were only a tenth of the people allowed into the city? (v. 1)

   Jerusalem was in ruins and had to have houses rebuilt. If Nehemiah allowed everyone who wanted to return to the city into the city, the rebuilding would have failed. There was not enough food or shelter for the once large population of the city. As the city rebuilt, more people could live in Jerusalem.

2. Why were people blessed for living in Jerusalem? (v. 2)

   This verse is implying that not all the people selected in the tithe returned to the city. With the city destroyed, it would have been a problematic existence. Cities in Nehemiah's day were crowded and overpopulated. Many of them elected to live in small towns. In addition, the people were farmers. It is difficult to impossible to run a farm in the city.

3. What is the meaning of verse seventeen?

   This verse is a Semitic idiom which means "that one who fails to admonish his fellow bears the other's sins as if he had transgressed himself." [38]

4. Why was Nehemiah angry at his fellow Hebrews who married pagan women? (v. 25-30)

   Nehemiah knew that Judah and Israel's problems were a result of marriages to foreign women. This practice needed to stop if the people who returned to Jerusalem remained as a consecrated people to the LORD.

---

[38] Nosson Scherman and Meir Zlotowitz, *The Writings = Kesuvim / The Writings: with a Commentary Anthologized from Rabbinic Writings = Ketuvim: 'im Perush Rashi, Metsudat Dayid, Metsudat Tsiyon, ye-'od* (Brooklyn, NY: Mesorah Publications, 2016).

Biblical Personalities/Peoples

1. Tyrians (v. 16) were people who lived in the city of Tyre.

2. Moabites – "member of a West-Semitic people who lived in the highlands east of the Dead Sea (now in west-central Jordan) and flourished in the 9th century BC. They are known principally through information given in the Old Testament and from the inscription on the Moabite Stone. The Moabites' culture is dated by scholars from about the late 14th century BC to 582 BC, when, according to the Jewish historian Josephus (1st century AD), they were conquered by the Babylonians."[39]

3. Ashdodite were people who came to Jerusalem from the city Ashdod.

Culture Section

Questioning the passage

1. What day is being referred to in verse one?

This day was the day that the wall of Jerusalem was consecrated.

2. What is the book of Moses? (v. 1)

The Sages believe that the book of Moses is Deuteronomy. This book is written in first person singular. It is considered a final "sermon" by Moses to the children of Israel.

---

[39] "Moabite," Encyclopædia Britannica (Encyclopædia Britannica, inc.), accessed May 6, 2021, https://www.britannica.com/topic/Moabite.

3. Why were the foreigners removed from the site that the Book of Moses was read? (v. 3)

   The Amorites and Moabites were considered enemies of Israel. Each nation had attacked Israel over the years. Therefore, Nehemiah believed that they should not be blessed by the words of the Book of Moses.[40]

4. Why were the merchants set up next to the wall? (v. 20-21)

   Merchants would set up tables next to the wall in Jerusalem on Friday towards the evening. Then they waited for the city gates to be opened. The people in Jerusalem could then buy their wares. However, Nehemiah believed that this practice violated the Sabbath codes. Therefore, the merchants were threatened with physical harm if they continued this practice.[41]

Thoughts

Nehemiah was concerned about the people returning to Adonai worship as he was in overseeing the wall's completion in Jerusalem. Nehemiah wanted the people to become consecrated to the LORD. The people had to let go of all the pagan influences that had infected them. If they did not, then they would not have the protection of the LORD. The people lived in Babylon for seventy years. They picked up some of the practices of the Marduk (the god of Babylon) cult.

---

[40] Nosson Scherman and Meir Zlotowitz, *The Writings = Kesuvim / The Writings: with a Commentary Anthologized from Rabbinic Writings = Ketuvim: 'im Perush Rashi, Metsudat Dayid, Metsudat Tsiyon, ye-'od* (Brooklyn, NY: Mesorah Publications, 2016).
[41] IBID.

Bibliography

"Ammonite." Encyclopædia Britannica. Encyclopædia Britannica, inc. Accessed April 24, 2021. https://www.britannica.com/topic/Ammonite.

"Ashdod." Wikipedia. Wikimedia Foundation, April 5, 2021. https://en.wikipedia.org/wiki/Ashdod.

Bible Map: Hakkephirim (Ono). Accessed April 26, 2021. https://bibleatlas.org/full/hakkephirim.htm.

Errico, Rocco A., and George M. Lamsa. *Aramaic Light on Ezra Through the Song of Solomon*. Smyrna, GA: Noohra Foundation, 2010.

"Geshem the Arabian." Wikipedia. Wikimedia Foundation, November 14, 2020. https://en.wikipedia.org/wiki/Geshem_the_Arabian.

GotQuestions.org. "Home." GotQuestions.org, August 14, 2007. https://www.gotquestions.org/Ammonites.html.

GotQuestions.org. "Home." GotQuestions.org, November 29, 2017. https://www.gotquestions.org/Artaxerxes-in-the-Bible.html.

"Hachaliah." Wikipedia. Wikimedia Foundation, September 12, 2020. https://en.wikipedia.org/wiki/Hachaliah.

"Hanani Definition and Meaning - Bible Dictionary." biblestudytools.com. Accessed April 22, 2021. https://www.biblestudytools.com/dictionary/hanani/.

Harris, R. Laird, Gleason L. Archer, and Bruce K. Waltke. *Theological Wordbook of the Old Testament*. Chicago: Moody Press, 2004.

The Institute for Creation Research. Accessed April 22, 2021. https://www.icr.org/books/defenders/2489/.

"Judah." Encyclopædia Britannica. Encyclopædia Britannica, inc. Accessed April 22, 2021. https://www.britannica.com/topic/Judah-Hebrew-tribe.

"Moabite." Encyclopædia Britannica. Encyclopædia Britannica, inc. Accessed May 6, 2021. https://www.britannica.com/topic/Moabite.

"Moses." Encyclopædia Britannica. Encyclopædia Britannica, inc. Accessed April 22, 2021. https://www.britannica.com/biography/Moses-Hebrew-prophet.

Murai, Hajime. "Literary Structure (Chiasm, Chiasmus) of Book of Ezra and Nehemiah." Literary structure (chiasm, chiasmus) of each pericopes of Book of Ezra and Nehemiah. Accessed April 26, 2021. http://www.bible.literarystructure.info/bible/15_EzraNehemiah_pericope_e.html.

Robin. "Noadiah: The Lost Prophetess." Robin Cohn, September 20, 2010. https://robincohn.net/noadiah-the-lost-prophetess/.

Rosenberg, A. J. *Daniel, Ezra, Nehemiah: a New English Translation = Sifrê Dānîyyēl, 'Ezrâ, Neḥemyā.* New York: Judaica Pr., 1991.

Scherman, Nosson, and Meir Zlotowitz. *The Writings = Kesuvim / The Writings: with a Commentary Anthologized from Rabbinic Writings = Ketuvim: 'im Perush Rashi, Metsudat David, Metsudat Tsiyon, ve-'od.* Brooklyn, NY: Mesorah Publications, 2016.

Software, Logos Bible. "Tobiah (Ammonite)." Biblia. Accessed April 22, 2021. https://biblia.com/factbook/Tobiah-(Ammonite).

"Susa." Wikipedia. Wikimedia Foundation, April 19, 2021. https://en.wikipedia.org/wiki/Susa.

End Notes

---

[i] Sanballat, Tobiah, and Geshem were three enemies of the Jews who made several attempts to stop Nehemiah from rebuilding the walls of Jerusalem. Sanballat and Tobiah are first mentioned in Nehemiah 2:10 as upset about Nehemiah's work: "When Sanballat the Horonite and Tobiah the Ammonite official heard about this, they were very much disturbed that someone had come to promote the welfare of the Israelites." In verse 19, they, along with Geshem the Arab, mock Nehemiah, saying, "What is this you are doing? . . . Are you rebelling against the king?" When the construction was taking place, their anger grew: "When Sanballat heard that we were rebuilding the wall, he became angry and was greatly incensed. He ridiculed the Jews" (Nehemiah 4:1; cf. verse 7).

[ii] Meïr Leibush ben Yehiel Michel Weisser (Malbim) was a rabbi, Hebrew grammarian, halachic scholar, and author of one of the most insightful and comprehensive Torah commentaries since medieval times. Known as the "ilui (prodigy) of Volhynia," he served in seven different rabbinic posts over the course of his lifetime. His staunch adherence to halacha and defense of tradition put him in direct confrontation with "enlightened" intellectuals who wished to introduce Reformist innovations in worship and other communal institutions. While serving as chief rabbi of Bucharest, he was falsely charged by his opponents and he only escaped imprisonment on the condition that he leave Romania. Persecution by reformers followed him to other rabbinic posts, including Lunchitz, where he was additionally attacked by a Chassidic faction that accused him of introducing enlightenment thought in his Torah commentary. On his way to accept a post in Krementchug, he fell sick in Kiev and died on the first day of Rosh HaShanah. Source: https://www.sefaria.org/person/Malbim

---

iii Rabbi Solomon ben Isaac (Shlomo Yitzhaki), known as Rashi (based on an acronym of his Hebrew initials), is one of the most influential Jewish commentators in history. He was born in Troyes, Champagne, in northern France, in 1040.

At age 17, Rashi received an education in the yeshiva of Rabbi Yaakov ben Yakar in Worms, where the "Rashi Chapel" was built years after his death (this chapel was subsequently destroyed during the German occupation in World War II, and rebuilt in 1950). At age 25, he returned to Troyes, where he became a rabbi. Since rabbis were not yet paid officials at this point in time, Rashi also worked with his family in the local vineyards. In 1070, he founded a yeshiva where he taught many disciples, some of whom would also go on to become prominent Jewish scholars. In 1096, Rashi witnessed the massacre of friends and family members at the hands of Crusaders en route to the Holy Land. He died in 1105 in Troyes. Source: https://www.myjewishlearning.com/article/who-was-rashi/

iv "According to tradition, God judges all creatures during the 10 Days of Awe between Rosh Hashanah and Yom Kippur, deciding whether they will live or die in the coming year. Jewish law teaches that God inscribes the names of the righteous in the "book of life" and condemns the wicked to death on Rosh Hashanah; people who fall between the two categories have until Yom Kippur to perform "teshuvah," or repentance. As a result, observant Jews consider Rosh Hashanah and the days surrounding it a time for prayer, good deeds, reflecting on past mistakes and making amends with others." Source: https://www.history.com/topics/holidays/rosh-hashanah-history

www.ingramcontent.com/pod-product-compliance
Lightning Source LLC
Chambersburg PA
CBHW081145130726
47996CB00009B/2998